How to Write

for the

Juvenile Market

How to Write
for the
Juvenile Market

by

Marjorie M. Hinds

Frederick Fell, Inc.

New York

To the memory of

Dorothy

who even in my earliest attempts

at writing was my critic, counselor,

and comrade.

CONTENTS

How to Write

for the

Juvenile Market

Chapter 1

SURVEYING
THE JUVENILES

Writing for young people is one of the most satisfying tasks in the world. Not only is the reaction from one's readers rewarding, but the writer senses a sort of magnetism between himself and the hundreds of young people who read his work.

Now if you are interested in becoming a juvenile writer, and we assume that you are or you'd not be reading this page, you should take a careful survey of both this particular field of writing and your own qualifications for it. This chapter deals primarily with what the field itself has to offer.

A quick glance at our crowded kindergartens and public schools reveals an ever-increasing number of young readers. Those readers must depend upon people dedicated to the job of writing for them. As a result, hundreds of new children's books and thousands of juvenile magazine stories are published each year. Several hundred editors are constantly on the alert to discover authors, while their desks are piled with manuscripts from "hopefuls." Unfortunately, most of those stories miss the mark because the would-be authors have not realized they were competing in a specialized field.

Now the best proof that you can write successfully is the editor's check. And one good reason for believing that you will succeed is the fact that you have turned to juveniles. Why? There are several reasons.

The juvenile field is a *valuable training ground* for the writer looking for his first sale. The competition here, while not to be underestimated, is slight in comparison to that for the slicks. Many a writer starts by writing magazine stories and then goes to other work. For instance, some stories for the very young that have been published in juvenile magazines may prove suitable, with minor changes, for book publication. Serials are also frequently expanded into juvenile books. Or one may go on to adult writing where he will find his experience invaluable, especially if his stories involve young characters.

The writer who likes children and likes writing for them can find a *ready market*. Many people earn a very good living by writing alone, but earning ability comes slowly, as it does in any other vocation. Not that you'll get rich in this field, though of course, books are more remunerative than magazine stories and often pay royalties for many years. And even if your returns in the book field don't rate with a best seller, the average juvenile is almost sure to pile up more impressive sales than the average novel *not* on the best selling list. Remember that a juvenile goes on selling year after year, providing the author a steady income, and is kept in print far longer than adult fiction.

The juvenile magazines pay lower rates but they are *steady* and do not change in style and requirements as do adult magazines. The market is a friendly one, with editors eager to help the beginner and equally interested in the best manuscripts they can find. Once established, and you have become known in your field, you will find regular markets where you can repeat with more sales, thus cutting down on time and risk.

Nearly 100 weekly publications, many of them representing various religious denominations, are depending almost entirely upon free-lance writers to supply their needs. And even if one finds himself selling only to the 1¢ and 2¢-a-word rate papers at first, he can, by working in volume, build up for himself a comfortable little side income. In addition to standard juvenile markets, farm papers and daily newspapers often provide space for juvenile material. Surely the beginning writer is wise to choose the *largest market of all* for his first hurdles.

But we must not make the mistake of thinking that because we are writing for children, we do not necessarily have to put forth our best efforts. On the contrary, turning out acceptable juvenile writing is as difficult a task as a writer can set for himself. It is not an easy wedge by which one tries to force his way to literary fame. It is not an apprenticeship to writing for adults. It is a craft of its own, with requirements of its own. You simply cannot put articles and stories together haphazardly and hope to be paid for them. Those children toward whom you are going to direct your writing are intelligent little beings; they can spot stale and life-less stuff just as readily as editors of children's pub-lications can. Our willingness to accept this truth will mean the difference between "Sorry" from the editor and "Enclosed find check."

We have for the most part emphasized the commercial side of writing for young people. But there are other rewards, too. For one thing, there is a certain inner joy that comes from knowing that what we have written has *pleased* children. And before it can please children, it has had to pass the scrutinizing eyes of an editor, possibly a librarian, and most likely a parent.

Then there's the challenge that comes when we realize that what we write has a pronounced effect upon the minds of our readers. Adults are already developed, their standards already established when the writer gets to them. They are more likely to take issue with a book or a magazine article and label it poor, simply because they disagree with it, than to consider the facts unbiasedly and take stock of their own opinions. Fortunately, not all adults are alike, but most of us cling rather stub-bornly to our views—whether right or wrong.

Youngsters, though, are still being molded. What we write for them can have a permanent influence upon their thinking. They are sensitive to change, enthusiastic about it. There is an eagerness to improve, to learn a better way. The juvenile reader automatically identifies himself with the child in the story or article. Therefore, as he follows the experiences, mistakes, new contacts with life, and perhaps a bit of the growing up process of the child character, the youngster himself absorbs these details and is being educated. And after all, if we can lead that child one small, hesitant step toward maturity and understanding, without its appearing so, we have educated him. Surely this privilege as a writer should incite nothing but our best efforts.

We have up to this point shown you what the juvenile writing field offers—its scope, its responsibilities, its rewards. Now let's look at you, the writer. We have established only one fact, that you want to write and write successfully. That in itself is a start. But what about your further qualifications?

Basically, you should possess four. To begin with, you *should genuinely love children.* Not because you're trying to launch a career where they figure in a big way, but because you love them for *themselves.* You, as a writer, must respect your reader audience whether they are six or sixteen.

You should, if you do not have children of your own, *cultivate an acquaintance* with as many as possible. It may mean visiting playgrounds, nursery schools, the swimming pool, the corner sweet shop. Plan to spend some time with or near them; study them; observe their likes and dislikes. Only in these ways can you sympathize with them or understand them. Remember, you cannot fool young people. And just as a child reads the heart from a facial expression, so he senses from written words whether the author is genuinely interested in him and in the story for him.

You must possess some *natural writing ability*. Probably because we are all taught at an early age to put words on paper, we are likely to think that is all there is to it. But it's more than that. What we have to say may be highly interesting but if our manner of telling it is *not* interesting, our chances of succeeding are poor. To make the best use of your story material, you should develop a style that is clear and simple, with a careful choice of that word or phrase best suited to carry your exact meaning. An average knowledge of correct English grammar is, of course, included in this requisite. Loving your subject and your reader, you will write with enthusiasm and spontaneity. You may find for a time that you lose the fluency that was yours as you transfer the ideas from mind to paper. However, if you really want to write, don't let this awkwardness frighten you. Acquiring a skill is never simple.

Perhaps the thing a writer needs most is *grim determination*. You will have to be willing to hang on in the face of repeated rejection slips. There will be many occasions when you'll pull the last page of your "brain child" excitedly from the typewriter, convinced that "This is it!" only to discover later that an editor has signaled "thumbs down." You will need patience to rewrite, revise, and wait for editors' decisions. Craftsmanship is a process of untiring labor, of smoothing out rough spots, of taking pains over endless details.

Is it all worth the effort required? By all means, yes! It is no light thing to enrich the child's world with something he wants and needs. If you have a real bent for writing for young people, you'll not consider one phase more important than another. You'll write because you want to. You'll have your share of defeats, discouragement, and disappointment. But you'll stick with the task, and some day after one of your stories has fallen into a pair of little admiring hands, you're going to hear some little fan say, "Boy, that story was 'perfeck'!"

Chapter 2

KEYS TO THE CRAFT

No matter how good a teacher is, there is no one who can impart the actual gift of writing to his students. But those who *can* be developed into writers do experience a decided urge to write and are eager, with the fundamental ability that they have, to develop it. Remember, writing is a business like any other. And in preparing you for that business, we can show you what *not* to do; we can demonstrate techniques that probably you knew nothing about; and we can help you develop creative power that you never sensed was yours.

It seems reasonable that upon engaging in *any* kind of work a person should expect to learn certain tools of the trade. And yet I believe that many regard a typewriter, some paper, a few original ideas, and a little natural writing ability as all the equipment writers need.

There are certain very definite "keys to the craft" that every writer should employ. The first is that of *reading*. Oh, I now that the average would-be writer is so eager to use his pencil that he doesn't want to use his eyes. He's perfectly willing to recall, though vaguely, the stories he enjoyed as a child—*The Christmas Carol, Rip Van Winkle,* and others. But recalling them is not reading them, and I'm not necessarily talking about stories that were written a hundred years ago anyhow. When Francis Bacon wrote "Reading maketh a full man . . . writing, an exact man," he certainly sensed the vast influence of the printed page upon people's lives.

Your reading has a definite bearing upon your writing. The editor, like the teacher, can invariably detect the difference between the "reader's" achievement and that of the "non-reader's." This does not mean that we should imitate a particular author, nor that the subject matter should be someone else's. But it does follow that the greater a storehouse one can unconsciously draw from, the more color and substance the writer can evolve for his own expression. And that storehouse is filled in no other way than by *reading, reading, reading!* That is what an early writer meant when he said, "There is creative reading as well as creative writing."

Authors who aim to reach boy and girl readers should acquaint themselves with the book shelves of a children's library. There they can observe the worn copies—the best advertisement I know of for successful books—as well as those which have gathered dust. The librarian herself can be of great assistance. From her wide experience with young readers she can tell you exactly what stories have appealed to youngsters, what ones have been passed up. Browsing through some such book as *History of Children's Literature* and studying its comments often serves as an eye-opener, too. In passing, let me urge you strongly to use every spare moment you have to acquaint yourself with reading material that has made a record of its own among the juveniles. Writing, then, means studying, analyzing, remembering, learning—at the same time recognizing the trend of public likes and dislikes.

The second key to writing success is *a time schedule*. It may seem impossible for you to set aside a certain hour of every day for plotting, collecting facts, or actual writing; and yet from the very start you should take this writing business seriously enough to warrant setting aside at least one hour every day. If you can squeeze in more than one hour, all the better, but be true to it.

The proverbial statement "I'll bet I could write acceptably if I only had the time" is nonsense. You never *have* time. And you can seldom *find* it. It is something you *make*. And you make it by rearranging your present habits, pushing some things out of their customary places.

For most of us the creative life is something that has to be brought to full power by our own efforts and sandwiched in between earning a living at something else or home-making. But if the desire is great enough, you'll do it. Harriet Beecher Stowe, while taking care of a home and children, turned out *Uncle Tom's Cabin* and in longhand, at that. Library shelves today are filled with works by part-time authors.

For one who writes, there are really never

enough hours. But since writing is work, it merits
a certain routine on our part. To get the most out
of the hours available, apply to yourself a simple
little time-management course. Arrange your duties
so that nothing, ordinarily, interferes with them.
Experiment, if you are a beginning writer, with
the time of day you think such a system will fit
your needs most efficiently. Maybe it will mean getting up an hour earlier in the morning or fitting in
an hour at the desk every night. It may mean
foregoing bridge or lodge or some other pleasure.
But whatever it is, once your habit is firmly established, when that time comes, you will *want* to
write. The busy housewives who are most successful at free-lance writing are those who have, amid
the confusion, and sometimes chaos, of a busy home,
managed to salvage an hour or two from their full
day and stick to their time-budget religiously. The
same is true of factory workers, farmers, office
workers, and others. Every one of them probably
hopes to reach that happy state where writing will
earn more than the job, so they can relinquish the job
and "find time to write."

After all, it is the daily pegging away, whether
on full or part time basis, that results in achievement and an increasingly inspired performance.
After you have reached the actual writing stage, you
should so budget your time as to allow no fewer
than 500 words a day. A person with a little talent
and a lot of ambition can achieve far more than a
gifted person who is unwilling to work hard or
regularly.

You must determine, from your time budget,

when you can work and when you can't, and for
how long at each opportunity. You will find, if
you do make such a budget, that it's no easier to
keep than a financial one. And yet, by the mere
attempt at it, and the effort to observe it, you will
find help in getting more done than you would
otherwise.

The third "key" to the craft of writing is the
possession and constant use of a *notebook*. The
human memory can be a remarkable storehouse from
which to draw, but something in black and white
is far more practical. From the very start, keep a
notebook and pencil handy with you all the time.
Make it a habit, not a "when-you-feel-like-it" urge.
It's a practice that every writer sooner or later
must adopt if he's to do anything worthwhile.

Too many writers wait until they get into the
middle of a story or article before jotting down
details, thereby losing sight of the embryonic germ
they meant to record. These jottings may consist
of anything or everything which stirs your imagination. They may be classified to fit your personal
needs such as dialogue, character, background, conversation overheard. As we discuss later in the book
the subject of finding ideas for writing, you will
see just how imperative your notebook habit can
be.

Not less important than the notebook is your
clipping file, especially usable as a backlog for article
writing. For this you may use manila folders or
even those made from sturdy wrapping paper.
Alphabetize the folders for the various types of

articles and ideas, as well as for features of writing skill that you need for reference. For instance, when you come across in your reading a particularly good beginning or a title or dialogue, slip that portion of the published article into the proper folder. As the clippings begin to accumulate, the folders should be filed in some container, such as an open cardboard box.

It is quite important that you maintain a wide and careful reading and clipping program to keep the ideas flowing in. These should be marked and filed while they are still fresh in mind.

As a juvenile writer, you will find that some magazines for children appeal to you more than others. You will read their contents and wish often that you had been fortunate enough to have written them. Clip those entire articles and stories and enter them in your file for ready reference. At the outset, you may want to classify articles in some such way as I have found workable:

1. personality sketches
2. how-to-make
3. how-to-do
4. biography
5. science
6. narratives in first person
7. travel
8. narratives in third person

In conclusion, I would suggest another valuable "key" to writing success—a reliable *writers' magazine.* In order to keep up to date, every professional person, whether he is a teacher, clergyman, or plumber, subscribes to the medium offered in his field for the betterment of his job. It would be illogical for the writer to think he is any different and cannot profit by the guidance and experience of others. For a nominal sum, such magazines put him in touch with technical articles by experts, market tips, regular lists of publications buying juvenile material, together with discussions of fellow craftsmen.

It is obvious, then, that the writer has at hand a variety of keys which are his for the mere taking. Don't lose them, but use them, and unlock the door leading to success!

Chapter 3

YOUR READER AUDIENCE

The word *juvenile,* as applied to the reader audience, covers a field of interest from early childhood to college level. Up to this point perhaps you've never classified young readers according to age. And it may be that you, like many others at first, do not have any particular leaning toward one group. On the other hand, maybe you do know exactly the age for which you'd like to write. If that is the case, your problem is already simplified.

The juvenile reader audience divides itself roughly into four age brackets. And you as a writer must know those age brackets and the specific interests and range of experiences in each. Basically, they are classified this way:

1. Tiny Tots   (from pre-school children to 9-year-olds)
2. Juniors   (9-12)

  3. Intermediates   (12-15)
  4. Teen-Agers and   (16-19)
     Young Adults

In a few cases certain magazine editors specify that their readers' ages are 13-14; others include those ages with 15-18. The boundaries for these groups, you see, are not rigidly fixed and there is a great deal of overlapping. But the classifications here are arrived at by the average run of editors, because there has to be an arbitrary division in the publishing program.

Many writers find that they can approach one group better than another. Some, though in the minority, have tried all four with equal success. Each writer has to decide for himself the particular age bracket for which he wishes to write, this decision being based upon his own knowledge of children at that age, his experience with them, and an aptitude for approaching that group more successfully than another.

It is safe to say, though, that the best writer does not attempt to succeed at all four. He chooses one, studies that group carefully, makes personal contacts with children of that age, finds out their likes and dislikes and what they read, listens to them talk, and then adopts the procedure recommended for his choice. In other words, *he must know his readers.*

Each group has certain advantages and disadvantages. Each has its problems. In later chapters as you study them separately, you will realize the

potential within each one as well as the requirements on your part.

Let me urge you to be unbiased in your choice
of reader audience. Do not eliminate, for instance,
the chapters dealing with tiny tots and juniors, simply because you've made up your mind to write for
teen-agers. By studying the material pertaining to
the first, putting forth your best efforts, and following the suggestions religiously, you can and probably will produce acceptable work. But moving on
to another group, and doing likewise, you may discover that this age has even a greater appeal, and
so forth. While the principles of good writing may
essentially be the same, whether the reader is six
or sixteen, much depends on our ability and readiness to adapt ourselves to those ages. The fact that
I have written and sold for every age group still
entitles me to a preference, and in that preference
I do my best job and have the most fun.

Some teachers suggest to new writers that they
begin with short stories. They feel that this type of
writing can be a medium for experimentation in
how to write with brevity, how to plot, how to keep
a story moving. True, our initial labors may have a
lot more learning than earning in them, but the
day has gone by—if it ever really existed—when an
amateurish output of stories for children can yield
anything but rejection slips.

Writing for any age group does not confine
itself simply to story creation; it includes article
writing as well. Both are important in the children's
world. And so throughout the chapters that follow

you will find an even balance of emphasis between the two fields of writing.

Actually, from the standpoint of the writer, I've never been able to figure out why the amateur who has an acceptable command of English doesn't pull for article writing first. Never has he faced a more fact-conscious public; never have non-fiction rates been higher. Furthermore, never have we had "new name" writers of non-fiction breaking into slick magazines so readily and frequently. Yet we can't boast of very many beginning fiction writers hitting *Saturday Evening Post* or *This Week*. Unless the beginning writer is willing to face disappointment and the possibility of a long road ahead, even in juvenile writing, he should think twice before deciding story writing must come first, article writing later.

Once you have decided what type of writing you most want to concentrate on, don't make the next likely mistake—that of hitting too high! In other words, at the beginning stage, steer toward markets that pay minimum rates. After all, you're only in the process of learning your craft, and the slower, more cautious a road you travel, the surer you are of its being paved with favor.

And writing for the juveniles, whether it's fact or fiction, can serve as the springboard to better markets. It can be the testing ground, the laboratory, the basic training—call it what you will—to find one's self in the job of writing. Remember, no greater compliment can one receive than that of being a good writer for juveniles.

Now for preparation. You should by all means

first acquaint yourself thoroughly with the magazine field for juveniles. You should keep abreast of the current publications, especially those to which you hope to send contributions. A reliable writers' magazine, suggested earlier, supplies at various intervals throughout the year lists of marketing opportunities with up-to-the-minute requirements and rates offered. There are several splendid market guides, as well, that are published annually and contain invaluable information for authors.

To study such lists, however, is not enough. You would do well to send for sample copies of magazines and church papers for your own personal study. Form the habit, too, of consulting those that are available at public libraries and on newsstands.

It would be folly to think that any list compiled here would be absolutely correct for very long. The changes in editorial staffs, magazine policies, and current happenings enter into the needs of editors continually. Neither is any list an exhaustible one. The best that any instructor can do is to list the surest bets and remind you to keep alert for changes.

TINY TOTS

Catholic Youth, Salvatorian Center, New Holstein, Wisconsin

Child Life, 3516 College Ave., Indianapolis 5, Indiana

Children's Playmate, 6259 Union Ave., Cleveland, Ohio

Children's Stories, 240 W. Fifth St., Dayton 2, Ohio

Christian Science Monitor, 1 Norway St., Boston 15, Massachusetts

Hand in Hand, Augsburg Publishing House, 426 S. Fifth St., Minneapolis, Minnesota

Humpty Dumpty's Magazine, 52 Vanderbilt Ave., New York 17, New York

Jack and Jill, Independence Square, Philadelphia 5, Pennsylvania

News Trails, Scholastic Magazines, 33 W. 42nd St., New York 36, New York

Our Little Messenger, 38 W. Fifth St., Dayton, Ohio

Pictures and Stories, 201 Eighth Ave., Nashville 2, Tennessee

Primary World, Winona Lake, Indiana

Steps, Augsburg Publishing House, 426 S. Fifth St., Minneapolis, Minnesota

Story Friends, Mennonite Publishing House, Scottdale, Pennsylvania

Storyland, P. O. Box 179, St. Louis 3, Missouri

Stories for Children, 1200 E. Fifth St., Anderson, Indiana

Stories, 930 Witherspoon Bldg., Philadelphia, Pennsylvania

Storytime, 127 Ninth Ave. N., Nashville 3, Tennessee

Story World, American Baptist Offices, Valley
Forge, Pennsylvania

Together, P. O. Box 423, Park Ridge,
Illinois

Wee Wisdom, Lee's Summit, Missouri

JUNIORS

Adventure, 127 Ninth Ave. N., Nashville 3, Tennessee

Aim Higher, 262 E. Fourth St., St. Paul 1, Minnesota

Boys and Girls, 240 W. Fifth St., Dayton 2, Ohio

Calling All Girls, 52 Vanderbilt Ave., New York 17, New York

Children's Friend, The, 33 Richards St., Salt Lake City, Utah

Covenant Trails, Covenant Press, 5101 N. Francisco Ave., Chicago 25, Illinois

Family Herald, 245 St. James St., W., Montreal 1, Quebec

Friendways, 1303 E. Fifth St., Anderson, Indiana

Highlights for Children, 968 Main St., Honesdale, Pennsylvania (send 50c)

Journeys, 1451 Dundee Ave., Elgin, Illinois

Junior Catholic Messenger, 38 W. Fifth St., Dayton 2, Ohio

Junior Hi!, 3558 S. Jefferson St., St. Louis 18, Missouri

Junior Life, 8100 Hamilton Ave., Cincinnati 31, Ohio

Junior Trails, 1445 Booneville Ave., Springfield, Missouri

Junior World, P. O. Box 179, St. Louis, Missouri

Juniors, American Baptist Publications, Valley Forge, Pennsylvania

My Counsellor, 1825 College Ave., Wheaton, Illinois

News Explorer, Scholastic Magazines, Inc., 33 West 42nd St., New York 36, New York

Story Trails, Light and Life Press, Winona Lake, Indiana

Sunday Pix, David C. Cook Publishing Co., Elgin, Illinois

Trailblazer, 930 Witherspoon Bldg., Philadelphia, Pennsylvania

Trails for Juniors, 201 Eighth Ave. S., Nashville 3, Tennessee

Young Crusader, 1730 Chicago Ave., Evanston, Illinois

INTERMEDIATES

American Girl, 830 Third Avenue, New York 22, New York

Bible Truth, 1137 Noble St. S.E., Grand Rapids 7, Michigan

Boys' Life, New Brunswick, New Jersey

Catholic Boy, 908 Donmoyer, South Bend 14, Indiana

Catholic Miss, 908 Donmoyer, South Bend 14, Indiana

Co-Ed, 33 W. 42nd St., New York 36, New York

Datebook, 71 Washington Pl., New York 11, New York

Friends, 240 W. Fifth St., Dayton 2, Ohio

High, 5750 N. Ashland, Chicago 26, Illinois

Living Trails for Girls, 5334 W. Addison St., Chicago, Illinois

Onward, P. O. Box 1176, Richmond, Virginia

Progress, Lee's Summit, Missouri

Science World, Scholastic Magazines, 33 W. 42nd St., New York 36, New York

Straight, 8100 Hamilton Ave., Cincinnati, Ohio

'Teen Magazine, 5959 Hollywood Blvd., Los Angeles 28, California

Teens, American Baptist Publishers, Valley Forge, Pennsylvania

Teen Time, Light and Life Press, Winona Lake, Indiana

Teen Ways, Augsburg Press, 426 S. Fifth St., Minneapolis, Minnesota

Twelve/Fifteen, 201 Eighth Ave. S., Nashville, Tennessee

Upward, 127 Ninth Ave. N., Nashville 3, Tennessee

Venture, Christian Service Brigade, Box 150, Wheaton, Illinois

Venture, 930 Witherspoon Bldg., Philadelphia, Pennsylvania

Vision, P. O. Box 179, St. Louis, Missouri

Words of Cheer, Mennonite Publishing House, Scottdale, Pennsylvania

World Over, 426 W. 58th St., New York 19, New York

Young Ambassador, P.O. Box 233, Lincoln, Nebraska

Young Catholic Messenger, 38 W. Fifth St., Dayton 2, Ohio

TEEN-AGERS AND YOUNG ADULTS

American Farm Youth, 113 W. Main St., Danville, Illinois

Baptist Student, The, 127 Ninth Ave. N., Nashville 3, Tennessee

Christian Youth, 1816 Chestnut St., Philadelphia, Pennsylvania

Classmate, 201 Eighth Ave. S., Nashville, Tennessee

Conquest, 6401 The Paseo, Kansas City 30, Missouri

Covenant Youth Today, Covenant Press, 5101 N. Francisco Ave., Chicago 25, Illinois

Elizabethan, 2 Breams Bldg., London E.C. 4, England

Evangel, Winona Lake, Indiana

His, 1519 North Astor, Chicago 10, Illinois

Hi Way, 930 Witherspoon Bldg., Philadelphia, Pennsylvania

Horizons, 1451 Dundee Ave., Elgin, Illinois

Ingenue, 750 Third Avenue, New York 17, New York

Motive Magazine, P. O. Box 871, Nashville 2, Tennessee

One Magazine, Augsburg Publishing House, 426 S. Fifth St., Minneapolis 15, Minnesota

Power, 1825 College Ave., Wheaton, Illinois

Queen's Work, The, 3115 S. Grand Blvd., St. Louis 18, Missouri

Seventeen, 320 Park Avenue, New York 22, New York

Standard, 2923 Troost Ave., Kansas City 10, Missouri

Sunday School Times, 1211 Arch Street, Philadelphia, Pennsylvania

Teen Age, 529 Fifth Avenue, New York 17, New York

Young People, American Baptist Publishers, Valley Forge, Pennsylvania

Youth, Warner Press Inc., Anderson, Indiana

Youth for Christ, N. Main Street, Wheaton, Illinois

Youth's Christian Companion, 610 Walnut Ave., Scottdale, Pennsylvania

Youth's Comrade, 6401 The Paseo, Kansas City, Missouri

Some of the magazines and story papers, if not all of them, which are listed under each age group should be part of your personal equipment. You will find them splendid reference material as you study proper subjects, characterization, plot analysis, and later slanting for the juvenile market.

Most of the editors will be very cooperative. When making your request, enclose postage for mailing. Frequently you can save both time and money by asking for copies of three or even four published by the same press. For instance, the editors at 127 Ninth Ave. N., Nashville 3, Tennessee, have a magazine suitable for all four age levels: *Storytime, Adventure, Upward,* and *The Baptist Student.* Therefore one letter of request to this publishing house is all that is necessary, and probably for a dime you will be furnished with two copies of each paper plus an editorial brochure.

Some such note as this is sufficient and will save considerable time for the busy editor:

Dear Editor:

I should very much like to have you
furnish me with a sample copy of (list titles).
I wish to study them with a view to submitting
material in the future.

Postage is enclosed. Thank you kindly.

Sincerely yours,

Bear in mind it is not sufficient to use postcards for these requests, since the enclosure of postage is absolutely necessary. In a few cases you may find that the editors are a little slow in getting the copies off to you, but with the postage furnished them, they are definitely obligated to do so. (Note: *Child Life, Jack and Jill,* and others should be bought outright at a newsstand.)

When you find two or three papers that you like particularly well, and for which you'd enjoy trying submissions later, it will pay you to subscribe to those regularly. The fee is nominal compared with the value derived.

As soon as you receive your copies, classify them in folders according to TINY TOTS, JUNIORS, INTERMEDIATES, and SENIORS. This system is for ready reference and will save you much time later on.

Chapter 4

WHAT TO
WRITE ABOUT

Write about what you know!

For years we've been hearing those familiar words. And many aspiring writers have heard but not heeded. They prefer, it seems, to adopt their own trial-and-error method.

Obviously, it is easier for one to write about what he does know than about what he doesn't. Why, then, must we constantly be reminded of this fact when anything else would mean harder work?

The chief reason is this: The experience a person has had or the facts he is familiar with are so commonplace to *him* that the element of interest or romance seems missing. Those same experiences, though, could well be the very nuclei of stories or articles that the reading public is waiting for. Why write of the fantastic when reality is under our feet? Why delve into the realms of medieval chariot races, for instance, when the freckle-faced neighbor just won the scooter race for the fourth consecutive year? The writer can consume hours of time in study of his subject; he can pound away on his typewriter until the people below him move out; he can eliminate every trace of bad grammar from his manuscript and the finished work be a faultless specimen in arrangement; but unless he can present truth—as he sees it—about what he knows, his work will smack of superficiality.

That statement should not imply, however, that you cannot learn facts yourself and then present them. Nor does it mean that if you already know some facts about your subject, you can't read more about it, adding to your original fund of information. Of course you can.

Let me illustrate. On several occasions I had noticed a group of teen-age girls walking past my home with their arms full of hand-made articles. I became curious and called to them one day to inquire what they had been making. I have always been interested in art and handicraft, though my own talent along those lines is limited. From that interview, a self-imposed one on my part, I learned that a handicraft course had been recently organized for the teen-agers in town, that they were holding frequent classes, and that the project that week was finger painting, a trick that in reality is very simple yet provides a great deal of individuality from the members of the class. By further inquiry I discovered how they learned to finger paint; the length of time it consumed; what materials were used; what, if anything, had inspired the designs; and what articles they had constructed. (These included jewelry boxes, waste baskets, scrapbooks, etc.) With specimens of their work before me, I was sensing a growing interest in the subject myself. A trip to the library was my next move where I carefully took notes on all the material I could find. When I felt that I had done a reasonably good job on fact collecting and had acquired a general understanding of the procedure, I asked permission to visit the class and watch the group through the various stages. That, of course, was the most practical part of the whole thing, for the girls invited me to try my hand at it, and once again the old theory of "learning by doing" was substantiated. With several pictures of the finished articles which the girls displayed, my article, "Finger Fantasy," actually wrote itself a few days later.

You see, the only requisite I had for the whole article was a general interest in handicraft, then a specific interest in what I saw teen-agers doing, and the final interest in learning enough about it so that others, through my story, would enjoy it, too. And the research on it had become terribly fascinating in the bargain!

First of all, then, select a subject in which you are really interested. You don't have to be well versed in it, but you do have to be genuinely enthusiastic about it.

In story writing, as well, form the habit of drawing on everyday observations. Observe consciously the people and situations about you. Both articles and stories have so many points in common that it behooves you to consider each with an open mind and an eye ready to grasp at subjects suitable to either.

And so, we are now ready to discuss the second principle in writing for children, and that is:

Write about what children should know! (pertaining to article writing)

Article writing for children is a fascinating field. We have already discussed its sales possibilities as equal and perhaps better than those of stories in certain popular juvenile magazines, and though the pay is frequently small, it serves as a splendid avenue by which beginning writers can break into print. Furthermore, there is never that "waiting period" for a story plot to dawn; such an abundance of material is all about us that one need never run out of ideas! Besides, we must not forget that children are born with an inherent desire to learn.

There are, however, two pitfalls to avoid when directing articles toward young readers. The first is that of presenting material in such a way that the child senses he is being taught. No youngster will accept the cold, bare facts given him, but neither will he spurn them if they are dressed up in an inviting style.

The second pitfall is that of telling too much. Articles, unlike stories, cannot be absorbed in large doses. You may have gathered reams of material on a certain subject, all of which seems so terribly important to you that the article would be incomplete without it. Beware! You want the article read, don't you? Build it around one or two main incidents and then, if necessary, summarize briefly those other portions.

Articles, generally speaking, are of four types. The aim here is solely to introduce you to each kind with perhaps an identifying statement or two as we go along. Later we shall study the types individually, discussing the proper subjects for each at various age levels, how to secure interesting approaches, where to get material for them, and then analyze actual articles that have been sold.

1. Fact articles: those which contain information that children can profit by knowing, drawn from such fields as history, science, nature, religion, sports, vocations, character-building situations, travel, invention, industry, biography, geography, and the animal kingdom.

Fact articles are of two kinds:

(1) informative
(2) inspirational.

Many, of course, contain both qualities, but the aim in each should lean toward one particular element.

Let us see, for instance, in each of the categories above, which type we would likely develop and what subjects could be born from each of the general fields.

(a) History:—(informative)—Articles on such subjects as the first Thanksgiving; how the Bible came to China; history of old valentines; the daring ride of Marcus Whitman.

(b) Science:—(informative)—Articles on such subjects as seeds and leaves; watching weather at sea; the story of stones; reading thermometers; plans of scientists to travel to the moon, etc.

(c) Nature:—(informative)—Children are interested in honey bees; humming birds; marigolds and other flowers; the ingenuity of the ant; story of the locust; how certain flowers came to be state flowers; nature legends.

(d) Religion:—(inspirational)—These are usually of an editorial nature, prompted by such thoughts as "Lovest Thou Thy Neighbor?"; "Giving Our Mite"; "And the Greatest of These," but religious articles can be based on Bible facts or biography.

(e) Sports:—(informative)—Again, these can embrace no end of subjects including handball, archery, backyard balloon races for the little ones, football, sportsmanship.

(f) Vocations:—(informative and inspirational)—Articles on writing, teaching, the nursing profession, or almost any career young people find facing them today.

(g) Character-building:—(inspirational)—Challenging articles that will cause young people to stir themselves toward better living. For instance, "Share Your Christmas";

"Making the Most of Mother's Day"; or "Can You Say 'No'?"

(h) Travel:—(informative)—Articles based on visits to interesting places. "Let's Visit Palestine"; "The End of the Indian Trail"; "Safety With a Bicycle"; "The Canterbury Pilgrimage."

(i) Invention:—(informative)—Somewhat similar to the scientific, these can often present the story behind inventions that make a more forceful impression on young readers' minds than a mere encyclopedic account. "The World's Largest Telescope"; "Radios for Rovers"; "One-Man Helicopter."

(j) Industry:—(informative)—Articles giving the story of cotton, oyster farming, ship-building, diving for pearls, etc.

(k) Biography:—(informative and inspirational)—Human interest accounts of the lives of personalities young people should be familiar with. "Young Liszt"! "Only One Robert E. Lee"; "Lady With the Lamp" (Florence Nightingale).

(1) Geography:—(informative)—Here is a splendid opportunity to educate our readers as to customs in other lands, one world, natural resources, wonders of the world, ancient cities, culture, etc.

(m) Animal Kingdom:—(informative)— Children are devout lovers of animals, so here is wide open territory for the writer. Articles on America's funniest animals; training seeing-eye dogs; introduction to wild animals they should know.

(n) Hobby:—(informative and inspirational)—The older readers are especially interested in success stories, provided the hobbyist we use for our subject has done something out of the ordinary with his spare time, or has chosen for that hobby something off the beaten path.

2. How-to-do articles: those which explain in a clear, concise way the procedure a child can follow so that he, too, can learn and enjoy the activity explained. Subjects apply to such fields as entertainment, appreciation of the arts, and practical instruction. From these general headings let's see what topics we could easily arrive at for writing.

Entertainment, for instance, would boil down to such subjects as how to play a particular game, how to work a puzzle, how to stage a party that is different, how to start a coin collection, etc.

Appreciation of the arts might include such topics as how to read books and enjoy them, how to listen to good music, how to select colors that are becoming to you, how to judge a painting, how to make friends easily.

Practical instruction can be found in such helpful advice as how to work out a successful budget, how to study and enjoy it, how to be a better driver, what to do in certain emergencies, when to plant sweet peas, how to raise a flower garden without weeds.

3. How-to-make articles: presented in much the same way as the how-to-do, these articles must include a step-by-step procedure the child can follow in the construction of some object. The writer, of course, must understand every step of the process himself if he expects to teach successfully the construction to somebody else.

Subjects for such articles would include a vast variety, since all ages of both boys and girls are keenly interested in handicraft. A few possibilities might include how to make spool furniture, how to make a bow and arrow, how to appliqué aprons, how to spatter brush designs, how to construct a novel bird house, how to make vases from gourds, or how to make a scrapbook.

4. Profiles: those articles which by rights should be classified alongside biography, yet have become so distinctive themselves in the past few years that we choose to give them a conspicuous place here in our study. There's another reason, too. They are so universally popular among young readers (especially those in the 12-20 range) that they deserve considerable time spent on them.

The profile was originally a 300-500 word thumbnail biography. Today it can run to 1500 words (usually it is a little less) with an aim to present some interesting personality to the reader. It may be to show the many-sidedness of a teen-ager's ability; the success of a handicapped individual to fill his niche in life; the presence of some particular quality in a person that influenced his career. But whatever the aim, it is not to give a chronological account of that person's life—therefore should not be regarded strictly as biographical.

The third principle in learning what to write about is

Write about what children are interested in! (pertaining to stories)

Generally speaking, and it has to be general at this point for we are not breaking down yet to any certain age levels, children demand in their stories three basic elements: (1) they love suspense, (2) they insist (yes, even the youngest readers) that characters in stories be real, and (3) that their senses are acted upon (sight, smell, taste, sound, feeling).

Again—and generally speaking—we can say that children are fond of adventure, mystery, discovery, sports, excitement, and novelty.

But probably the best way to review the subjects they are interested in is by our own review of the things we enjoyed when we were small. (And don't ever think that unless those sense impressions of your own childhood are still keen that you can fit into the story-world for juveniles! Article writing may be your field instead.)

Let's go way back to our pre-school days and see if any of these thoughts recall experiences to us. Remember those fairy stories Grandma read? Or the lovely Bible tales in that huge, beautifully-colored picture book? And how about the pig that "puffed and puffed and blew the house down?" Yes, and those animal stories where Mr. Rabbit wasn't a rabbit at all but someone who lived over in the thicket and was keeping a close watch on Mr. Farmer's cabbage row. (It didn't matter to us, then, that the rabbit in the story had the supernatural ability of talking.)

And then as we grew older, we teased for that one about the hidden treasure; and "the poor little match girl" at Christmas; then came the ones about the Indians, the circus wagons, or maybe little Dick Whittington who dreamed of being Lord Mayor of London. And on and on.

Well, today, the children we write for have much the same interest at heart, even though the eight-year-old may seem far more advanced in our world than you think you were at the same age. They are still interested in parties, birthdays, playing store, going on picnics, wading, pets, watching trains, buses, and planes, playing with toys, running races. They still thrive on rivalry, excitement, and getting what they want. If, then, these are their interests, we as writers have the meat for the pie we're going to feed them.

As children grow a little older, they begin to show an interest in birds, in hearing about children their own ages living in other lands, the desire to earn money (lemonade booths and such), the "collecting" instinct.

Older yet, there has developed a vital interest in sports such as football, fishing, hunting, baseball; in the romantic epochs in history; life in other lands;

frontier life in our own country; careers; love interests; mystery; music; true life episodes; courageous
people; camp life; sacrifices on the part of heroes.

Later we shall show how some of these interests
can be developed into stories; also how to inculcate
the three necessary ingredients in them to insure
reader-interest and writer-sale.

Things to Do

At this point we suggest that you take a little
personal inventory in relation to the material already
covered. See if you can answer these questions
satisfactorily:

1. Why do so many writers refuse to write
   about things in their own back yards?
2. Does the writer necessarily have to be
   interested in his subject to do a good
   job?
3. Which form of writing (articles or stories)
   is becoming more popular than ever?
4. What are the two pitfalls to avoid in
   writing articles for children?
5. What two purposes has an author in
   writing articles?
6. Which type of article is usually of an
   editorial nature?
7. Must the writer of a how-to-do article
   know how to construct the object himself?

8. What is a profile?
9. What three elements must every juvenile story contain?
10. What measure can a person use to determine whether he is a writer of juveniles?

Make a list in your notebook of the types of fact articles that you are interested in. Then try to recall from your own experience facts, episodes, and practical knowledge of things you've read or been told about that you can list under each.

Make a list of how-to-do or how-to-make possibilities for future reference.

Just to practice logical thinking, list 1, 2, 3, etc. the various steps in making some object or following some procedure for a how-to article. It need be nothing new—perhaps a familiar child's game—but no matter how simple it is to you, assume that no one else knows how. The practice will help you to do straight thinking.

Begin making a list for profile subjects later on. Perhaps these thoughts will help you form that list: Is there a youngster or teen-ager or any interesting person in your community who has an unusual hobby? Is there someone who is "going places" in music? Do you know of someone who has made a large collection of rare things? Is there someone who has traveled in strange places? How about the many accomplishments of a blind person? Is there a seasonal function in your community that always calls for the ingenuity of a single person or a small group? Can you spot an individual who achieved when everybody else said it couldn't be done? A sacrificial soul? Can you get an inside story of some famous person? Is there a particularly successful business-man whose principles and methods are obviously the reason for that success?

If there are no children in your home, try to make casual contacts with those of various ages. Get in conversation with them; let them do the talking; lead them out. Find out their likes and dislikes, their interests, their problems, their attitudes. Form the notebook habit early; record suggestions, remarks now and then, so that later you will have something valuable to turn to.

Chapter 5

WHERE TO GET IDEAS

If you have been subscribing to writers' magazines or have read any of the countless books on writing technique, you probably have observed one very familiar sentence: Ideas are everywhere. It may be a shop-worn phrase, but let me urge you to take it literally and seriously. Even in creative writing classes we hear students say, "I'm completely out of ideas. Can you suggest where I should turn next?" Strangely enough, these words often come from individuals who have sold nearly all that they have written. How then, I wonder, can we make them realize that ideas are everywhere?

And then I remember that even Edwin Markham, our great peace-loving poet, was approached in his study one day by a dapperish young college graduate who urged the older gentleman to listen to his problem. He had all that it took to be a great writer, he assured Markham—vocabulary, polish, originality of style, and all the rest—but he couldn't think of any proper subjects on which to write! Markham eyed him closely for a moment, then slyly put his hand into his pocket, pulled forth a piece of string, and handed it to the aspiring young "genius." The budding poet's crestfallen face registered the blow of Markham's subtle rebuke.

Yes, literally and seriously, the "pieces of string" are all about us if we will only look for them. Let's examine some of the most common sources.

I. Be an "ear-eye-and-nose" specialist.

Too many of us have "eyes and see not; ears, and hear not." Personal observation can, if we are alert, supply us with a large percentage of our story and article ideas. But we need to form the habit of analyzing what we see and hear about us, and then "nose out" details for a story by means of query, research, or interview.

We must train our eyes to see what we look at. In the busy rush of living we have come to accept so passively what we travel past every day that our eyes do not focus on the "gold in the hills." The bazaars we attend; the style shows that are put on; the Thanksgiving party; the ending of a recent movie; the picture in the dentist's waiting room; all these, and hundreds more, can serve as eye-openers and check-cashers. Let me illustrate.

Visiting a scenic spot in the southern part of my home state a few years ago, I suddenly realized the seed for an article that should interest teen-agers. The occasion was a commemorative ceremony on one of the Civil War battlefields. Combining a few facts of the 1860's with those of the anniversary event resulted in "Vows of the Valiant" which I sold to a teen-age paper.

A photographer friend of mine showed me a picture one day in his children's collection, that of an adorable little girl sitting under her Christmas tree and holding up a toy phone to thank Santa. And although I admired the sweetness of the scene, my eyes focused on one of the most beautifully trimmed trees I had ever seen. I thought of the poet's line: "What tree so fair, so bright, so free?" and over me rushed the wild desire to "get going" on a Christmas tree article. Result? I was able to "nose out" some very interesting sidelights on Christmas tree history and received my check for "What Tree So Fair?" a few weeks later.

Watching three neighborhood youngsters at a sandpile and listening to their "problem"—that of planning what they could do to entertain the sick little girl across the street to compensate for their attending the circus—sent me quickly to my desk where a 1000 word story for tiny tots, "The Musical Kittens," (appearing in a later chapter) was finished in a few hours' time. True, I had eavesdropped to get my idea, but a sizeable check was forthcoming and welcome.

A casual question asked by a friend at a club meeting one evening alerted me to sudden writing action. One lady near me remarked that she understood "Nearer, My God, to Thee" had been played by our American bands more than any other hymn. Whereupon one of the other members asked, "Is it an American hymn?" The next spare moment I could muster for myself was used in reading the facts of the case. Amazed at the amount of material I found, I was equally interested in the "how-it-came-to-be-written" angle. So, "A Song is Born," published for teen-agers three months later, came about because a question had been asked and I had attuned my ears to it.

These are, of course, only a few of the many published articles prompted by just such simple, everyday happenings. They have been cited here at random only to demonstrate the privilege, yes, the obligation that is yours as a writer. On subways, in trains, stores, churches, at bridge, in conversation with friends, with the paper boy, with Johnny's teacher, with the plumber, or while walking to work, listening to TV or the radio, let *your* ears make money for *you,* too.

II. *The newspaper is the second vital source for ideas.*

A few years ago a very successful writer told me that for 108 articles he had written that year, 90% had sprung from ideas gleaned from daily newspapers. No, it does not mean that he stole anything; it means simply that by knowing how to read a newspaper, learning how to cull out the gems of human interest, and sensing the possibilities of those same gems as sparkling stories, writers have started tapping a source that is inexhaustible.

Furthermore, some have gone so far as to say that they dare not read but a page or two of a daily paper, the flood of ideas being so great that they feel overwhelmed rather than thrilled by such an abundance of material. Personally, I have followed the practice of listing all the ideas received from a single daily, then selecting the three that I feel most interested in developing for the particular market I have in mind.

Newspapers have the habit of relating the things the public is hankering for. Since the idea is the chief ingredient for a good article, we know that by using the newspaper method, then, writers are already past first base when they have spotted an attractive subject.

Now let's see how this plan works. And it really does work, for I am going to trace step by step as clearly as I can one of my own numerous experiences at newspaper "culling" and show you the results that came about.

I picked up a small town weekly one morning (before this I had always relied upon a daily paper) with my customary "What's-there-in-it-for-me?" frame of mind. On page one, way down in the right corner, I noticed an item headed: "Century Old Newspaper Reveals History of Local Interest." I read carefully and discovered that the owner of the paper was a speaking acquaintance of mine who lived about a mile from me. I called her at once, asking that I might borrow it for a day. Given her consent, I wasted no time in perusing it. The front page lead article hit me in the eye! A young Spaniard had just returned to New York with his fortune, a million dollars' worth of gold from the Great Valley, one year before gold was 'discovered' in California! The reason for his success had been a secret instrument, a magnetic goldometer, that proved to him that gold lay in the gorges of the mountains and not in the sand beds of the rivers as the natives believed. A three-column newspaper story in fine print held the complete information. All I had to do was to start off with a paragraph that would catch interest, rewrite the article in a somewhat fictional style by putting plenty of meat in the middle, dramatize the situation enough so that the reader would sense the reality of the thing, and I was all set. Finished, "Secret of the Hills" was definitely a boy's story and sold as just that. How would I ever have heard of Senor D'Alvear had it not been for a newspaper article?

I looked further. On that same page of my weekly I noticed a very short item with the humorous twist that a reporter often enjoys. It ran something like this: "Perfect Record in Blankville! Every registered Voter Turns Out at Polls—All 47!" But the next and last sentence of that tiny item was written for me! It stated that Blankville was the smallest borough in the United States. I readily jotted down in my notebook the real name of the town and planned my strategy. The town was forty miles away, but fortunately I knew one person who lived there. A contact, followed by a promise, made it possible for me to have in my hands page after page of the most fascinating details: how the little hamlet was established during the days of William Penn, that six families were the original Quaker settlers, the church (which still stands) was the first public building erected, what the reactions of the newcomers were as recorded in a diary preserved by a descendant living there today. Added to these, the length and width of the borough, the present day activity, mail service, and the industries followed there at present. Besides, I was able to make arrangements with a photographer for pictures of that little Quaker church, the village green, and other landmarks to accompany the article. In this type of writing, you see, research took the form of personal interview, questions, and visits; no encyclopedias or volumes of history could I turn to.

I looked on through the newspaper. This page three heading caught my fancy: "Blankville Athlete Amazes Crowd." I read on. The item was not among the sports articles. It was simply a three-paragraphed tribute to a high school lad who had, in spite of a severe physical handicap (the amputation of an arm), maintained a .300 hitting average in baseball. Teenagers are my own very particular interest, so naturally I clipped the item at once. In the next day's mail I submitted to the boy a request for information concerning himself, explaining that I was a writer and if he were willing, I should like to use that information in a magazine article. Receiving permission, I substituted a typed questionnaire to him.

Let me explain that in such cases I have found a questionnaire the only safe way (unless you actually interview) because you get what you want. A teen-ager would very likely omit details you were seeking, or perhaps emphasize something the public would slide over. To get an ample amount of information, though, my questionnaire had to be thorough and worded in such a way that I could have exactly what I needed. In response to my request, the boy's mother filled out the papers completely, at the end of which she added two or three little anecdotes that had sprung from his experiences while adapting himself to his condition after the accident. She even furnished me with negatives so that I could have the proper size gloss prints made to accompany the story. From there on, it was my job. In a later chapter I will show you the exact questionnaire, what I did with it, and how the newspaper item turned not into one sale, but three!

That was still not the end. I turned to the editorial page. One of the three topics dealt with what the editor called "a fast disappearing landmark in America." He was referring to the covered bridges dotting the countryside here and there on narrow, little-traveled roads. Though the editorial was brief, I believed I saw in it three statements sufficiently interesting to do some research on: (1) He had called it an American idea. (I wanted to read its history.) (2) It was fast disappearing in the United States, yet we could still boast of the 2000 remaining ones. (I wanted to know where most of them were, that is, if any special section of the

country had more than another. I became curious
about the longest one and the oldest one.) (3) And
he finished by arousing curiosity as to the mysteries
connected with the covered bridge. (That settled it.
I'd find out.) Perhaps my enthusiasm had been
whetted by the mere mention of the subject, for I'll
admit I thoroughly enjoy visiting antiquated things;
but I assure you that the preparatory work on that
article, "Rustic Retreats," and the writing of it was
really fun!

Besides, let me remind you, that because I followed the Newspaper method for ideas, I had culled
four subjects (six articles) and a substantial amount
of money out of one weekly.

III. Magazines, books, and pamphlets are full of story ideas.

Quite often, by skimming the pages of one
magazine, you can pick up an idea for another.
Again, it does not mean stealing the theme and
re-building it from an adult level to that of a
12-year-old's. It means simply studying the contents
of the magazine with your mind in a receptive,
imaginative mood and trying at the same time
to form comparable situations from your own
experiences.

For instance, as I was studying a juvenile magazine one day, I came across a story about the famous
"cross on the mountain"—in reality, the well-known
streams cutting across each other in the form of a

cross. I didn't read the story, in fact, never did—but I glanced at the picture illustrating the story. Through my mind flashed the thought of the famous monument on the boundary between Argentina and Chile and the story of how those two countries sought a lasting peace between themselves. I mused on how it could have any application to the present; whether there was anything in it for the juveniles; and, if so, what age it would appeal to. Then the idea dawned that the nations of the world today could well benefit by the same spirit that prompted the South American republics, swearing their peace at the feet of the Redeemer. I could not preach, for teenagers will not accept 'preachy' writing, but I could relate the story and show the significance of such a truce. "Christ of the Andes," suggested by a story in one juvenile publication, was sold to another.

Such experience can often come from reading books as well. It is not unlikely that many of our big-name writers get ideas from one another. In fact, we are told that one of the popular writers of today reads his contemporaries to fire himself into action! Even history books, with their already familiar events, can open new avenues to old themes if we strive to dig out the unusual, or the romantic, or the human interest side of those events.

I recall reading this in a sixth grade history one day: "Here at Fort Mandan, Lewis and Clark find an old French trapper whose Indian wife, Sacajawea, had been stolen years before from a tribe living in the Rocky Mountains. This trapper and his wife agree to take the explorers into the new country." The fact was certainly not new, would probably not be new to the average juvenile from 9 to 19. But somehow I couldn't help wondering if the Indian element, being the favorite that it is with youngsters, wouldn't warrant some work on a fictionalized article of that western expedition. I read the account as recorded in several history books, did some additional research, took plenty of notes, and gave myself up to it. The result was that an old history book story had taken on a new dress and my story, "Sacajawea," was published in one of the largest circulated periodicals for young people.

Often we little realize what a store of information is ours, as writers, in pamphlets that cost us nothing. There are literally thousands of them available for the asking. What a gold mine to the writer who is handicapped by the insufficient resources of a small town library!

The U.S. Time Corporation, Ingersoll Division, Waterbury, Connecticut, furnishes several interesting pamphlets on the story of time—surely a worthwhile and interesting subject for juveniles.

For years The Lincoln National Life Insurance Company, Fort Wayne, Indiana, has sent free on request a rather generous assortment of booklets on different phases of Lincoln's life, excellent for story and article ideas.

Information on Indians of today can be secured from Indian Rights Association, 301 South 17th Street, Philadelphia, Pennsylvania.

Levi Strauss and Company, Los Angeles, California, has material on old-time westerns guns and gun-fighters.

The U.S. Fish and Gamelife Service, Dept. of the Interior, Washington, D.C., can furnish any amount of information on fish and animals common in our country.

Everything from history of baseball to the making of a lead pencil, from historic Plymouth's history to proper care of the hair, is covered in hundreds of publications such as those mentioned above. Surely such a storehouse of ideas, filed systematically for tip-of-the-finger use, is an invaluable aid for any writer.

IV. Follow your lean!

Almost everyone has at least a single line that he's particularly good in; that is, he has, through an intense interest in or a natural knack for, acquired special knowledge of one subject. He may by profession have the inside track on some special phase of life that, if made use of effectively in writing, can reap for him a nice little income.

Perhaps, for instance, you're the best doll dresser in your community; the boy or girl scout leader for a local troop; an expert at handiwork; an assistant librarian; the kind of person that can make something out of nothing; a mechanical genius; an authority on dishes, guns, glass, or Currier-Ives pictures; one who is original in renovating furniture and rooms; a successful experimenter growing flowers, plants, rock gardens; an authority on birds and bird calls; on how to build a bird sanctuary; a student of astronomy; a successful cameraman; a minister or a registered nurse or a welfare worker.

If, by learning or doing something that has helped you gain any such special knowledge, you should be able to write and sell material based upon that knowledge. Again, let me cite some illustrations. I have been closely connected with writing for a good many years, having been a proof-reader for publishing houses, a high school English instructor, for several years, a contributor of stories and articles to many juvenile magazines, and author of several books. I have done ghosting, revision work, and have collaborated in the writing of a series of textbooks. Still I feel that my specialized knowledge lies in the field of teaching, and every time I find myself finishing a story or article, another looms before me waiting to be written—invariably born out of that teaching experience.

For instance, casting and coaching five high school girls in a one-act play one time was the beginning of a series of public appearances for them in their section of the state. Naturally I commercialized on the idea, so with a 1000-word story completed, accompanied by a gloss print showing the troupe in costume for one of their acts, "Thespians V" sold to a Canadian journal.

As the result of a vocabulary lesson one time I was amazed at the interest the students showed in the changes that had come about in our language during their own lifetime. Then we went back 25 years, 50, even a century. So fascinating did the study become for them that I knew it would be no risk for other teen-agers' interest. And I unconsciously had built the foundation for that very article, "What Time is Your English?" published a few months later.

In an advanced composition class one day we were experimenting with "sentence variety as a clue to effective writing." Not all the specimens submitted were superior, of course, but when I saw the vast improvement that had come about in many students' work, simply by following a few rules I had been hammering away on, I was forcibly convinced that here was something adult writers could profit by, too. "Variety is the Spice of Style," published in a nationally circulated writers' magazine, came about just that way.

Countless other "specialized knowledge" pieces have been given birth to as easily as those mentioned here. And just as many can be picked up in the experience of the housewife, the bricklayer, or the store clerk.

Things to Do

Make a list of ideas that come to you through being an "eye and ear" specialist.

Begin right now to study the newspapers that come into your home daily or weekly. Start a clipping file for your convenience.

Study magazines and books with your notebook open. Learn to read in to magazine contents your own adaptations for stories and articles.

After collecting subjects for each of the above, test each with these questions. If the subject can still stand up under this cross-examination, you are quite likely to have chosen wisely from observation, newspaper, book, or magazine.

a. Is the subject worthwhile?

b. Can you get adequate facts for it?

c. Will it have general appeal? (Avoid local news)

d. Does it have timeliness? (Or will it be out of date six months from now?)

e. Does it link with the present; that is, is there a current interest in such a subject?

f. Is the subject overworked? (Don't select one that's been hashed and re-hashed)

g. Do you see a possible market for it?

Chapter 6

WRITING FOR
THE TINY TOTS

Stories

To repeat the thought in an earlier chapter, unless we can recall our own childhood emotions and see through a child's eyes ourselves, we cannot hope to be a successful writer for little ones. The tiny tot group includes youngsters who need to be read to as well as those who can stand on their own. Youngsters of four have already acquired a story sense; they recognize that which entertains or stimulates them. Therefore, the first caution for us who aim to appeal to those little folk is to beware of relating only an incident when the story is the thing! The latter *must* include two things: (1) a cumulative interest and (2) something that happens.

Naturally, since the youngest of our readers have very immature minds, their story will of necessity have to be very simple. But the simplicity of that story does not excuse the writer from making use of those same two requisites. Children must know from the start what to look for and there *must* be action. If you have studied children, you realize only too well that they are busy little bodies—often to the point where we wonder how they can stand the pace. If love of action, then, is an inherent part of their nature, so must it be of the stories they enjoy.

Let us consider a few of the qualities that must necesarily be included in a tiny tot's story.

A. Time element Children cannot look beyond their noses. They are interested in NOW. They have little interest in the past. Moral for the writer? Make your story deal with the present!

B. Place At the earliest possible moment in the story, get the reader comfortably located. Whether our characters are raking leaves or swinging under the shady apple tree or making a jack-o-lantern at the kitchen table, we should have the curtain go up on that scene when the story is to begin.

C. Characters Very few in number, else the youngster becomes confused. By all means, have these characters children, preferably a boy and a girl or two of one and one of the other sex. The reason for this is that most magazines for youngsters 4-9 are designed for both boys and girls; and it is a veritable truth that girls will read about boys in a story, but boys do not like to read about girls only. By all means give each character a name at once; no "the little girl in the plaid dress" stuff. Unless it is absolutely necessary to help in the development of the story, one should not introduce an adult character.

Children play together, enjoy adventures together, talk naturally with one another, share experiences together—all during a "play time" without the presence of parents—so those same situations should be included in stories to make them true to life. One excellent plan is to make the characters in the story slightly older than the readers for whom they are intended, but do not specify the exact age of any!

D. The Subject This group thrives on animal stories, nature, and fanciful tales (particularly the tiniest ones); also legends, adventurous tales, true historical tales for the in-betweens; and for the older in the group, seasonal stories, true-to-life tales of simple science, adventure, and history.

E. Dialogue "Speak and we know your mood" can well be the motif for every bit of dialogue a writer puts on paper. If little Billy is really excited (and we know he will be) over the news that Uncle Jack is going to take him to the circus, what he says will show that excitement. It won't be any old "Oh, I'm glad!" but "Oh, goody. When do we start?" In other words, work first to see that the dialogue is natural. Then be sure that there are no long, dull speeches. Children are like many of us adults in that they interrupt each other. None of us can endure the long-winded fellow who could, if he would, boil 50 words down to 5. Tiny tots, as well, like to follow the story thread too well to wait for long speeches; and unless they are given what they want, they will skip part of the reading and get on with the rest of the story themselves. Be sure also that the dialogue is in keeping with the speaker. Mr. Wolf, for instance, will have a gruff voice and will display little mercy in his words. Certainly older sister Sue will call Becky to run the errand for her with still a different tone. No better means of revealing character can ever be sought than by careful selection of dialogue, and no more graceful a way to make the story progress.

F. Description Don't bore the child with scenic description. He won't read it anyhow. If we can get a picture across through action and conversation, we have done the ideal and the only right thing in presenting setting.

G. Action Almost everything that has been said about dialogue can be said about action. In fact, the two are so closely allied with each other that they by rights should be treated simultaneously.

For instance, when Billy heard he was going to the circus, the writer can use a double barrel to show the child's excitement in this way: "Billy clapped his hands eagerly. 'Oh, goody!' he cried. 'When do we start?'"

In my own writing classes I have been trying to break down the old theory that adjectives are picture words. I was taught, as were many of you, that adjectives describe subjects and therefore through their use we have a clearer picture of a person. It's not true. The power house for clear, photographic writing is the verb! A boy's eyes *widen* when he *spies* the rabbit; he *scrambles* into the thicket just as the injured bunny *hobbles* out of sight.

Don't misunderstand me. Well-chosen adjectives do have a place in a child's story. I am merely pointing out the over-emphasis we have given that part of speech. Surely we want the "fluffy yellow duckling" in our stories.

H. The Moral There is no more ticklish an angle to the business of writing a tiny tot story than that of the moral it contains. Certainly every story published in a Sunday School paper should be of a character-building nature. But to write so that some good quality of character is shown or some fine lesson conveyed without a finger pointing to a preachy text, is a task that comes by study, discernment, and practice.

We do not object to the child's absorbing a lesson and applying it to himself; that's what we do seek, in fact. But in no wise will our stories be accepted by an editor if there's a tacked-on "now-you-do-likewise" in evidence.

Plenty of good qualities can serve as meat for a wholesome little story without stress on the lesson itself. In the first story analysis shown later in this chapter Richie was rewarded for being kind to the strange little Swiss boy. Yet there is no sermon included; it was Richie's friend, Tom, who learned the lesson, the reader only profiting by it vicariously.

Our tiny tots can well afford to be shown the merits of honesty, loyalty, generosity, and all the others, but they will rebel against moralizing if they detect it.

Let's examine the construction on which a story is built. The real core of every story is, of course,

The Plot Literally, by the word *plot* we mean plan or a set pattern we establish for a story. Plot must be broken down into three parts:

(1) A story problem (presented as near the beginning of the story as possible)
(2) Efforts to solve that problem (solution to be made by the children in the story)
(3) Climax (Something must happen!)

Now let's analyze a plot according to these three elements, at the same time familiarizing ourselves more readily with the terms.

STORY PROBLEM:

Richie is greatly disappointed on the first day of school because the teacher assigns him to a seat beside a newcomer, a little Swiss boy, in order that Richie can help him. To make matters worse, she asks him to see that Karl is made to feel at home among the others.

EFFORTS TO SOLVE THAT PROBLEM:

Richie invites Tom, his best friend, to join him at recess to make the new boy welcome. Tom refuses. Baseball is more important. Richie, torn between duty to the teacher and the taunts of Tom to "come on and play and forget him," finally approaches the Swiss boy. Because Richie gives up his position as "third baseman" at recess to visit with Karl and because he shares a candy bar with the little homesick fellow, who at first can hardly swallow the candy for the lump in his throat, Karl soon responds with the same "give and take" attitude and shows Richie how to make a reed whistle.

CLIMAX:

When, on the following day, Richie has completed the task and proudly displays the new type of whistle to the other fellows, he is the envy of all the others. Not only is Karl received cordially on the schoolground but is soon inducted to the baseball nine's activities. We can rest assured the novel whistle is duplicated many times and that Richie's good turn served as a reminder to the others that kindness pays dividends.

And now let's study a specimen story and see how the various qualities, previously outlined as necessary, are incorporated in it.

INTRODUCTION
OF CHARACTERS

ACTION

STORY PROBLEM

IDENTIFICATION
OF NEW CHARACTER

The Musical Kittens

Becky looked up quickly from the sand-pile, her sunburned face brightening into a smile.

"Anne, just think! Tomorrow at this time we'll be starting for the circus!"

Anne, building a tunnel at the opposite end, said nothing. "Why, what's the matter?" her sister continued. "Aren't you excited? Dick says it's wonderful. He—"

"I'd like to see it, all right," interrupted Anne. "But—but, Becky, we can't go without Esther. She's been counting on it for weeks, and she's going to be so disappointed."

"I know," agreed Becky soberly. "It is a shame, but if she's careful now—like the doctor told her to be—she'll be well for school next year. And besides, we'll buy her something nice at the circus and tell her all about what we saw. Anyway, she wouldn't want us to stay—"

A familiar whistle suddenly announced to the girls that Dick was standing beside them.

"Oh, hello, Dick!" said Becky, smiling a big welcome to their favorite neighborhood playmate as she shaded her squint-

NATURALNESS OF
DIALOGUE

GROWING INTEREST

BIT OF
DESCRIPTION

HURRYING
THEME

ing eyes with her hand. "Did you have a good time at the circus yesterday?"

"Did I!" he said proudly. "Boy, what a parade! Bands, elephants, lions, 'n' everything!"

Anne's eyes grew wide with wonder. "And I suppose tigers and bears and snakes, too!"

"Oh, but you should see the monkeys!" Dick exclaimed. "They rode on the elephants' backs all during the parade. They'd run from one side to the other and wave at the people in the street just like we do. And then in the tent—"

Becky squealed loudly. "Oh, tell us all about it, Dick. But first, let's move over in the shade. It's getting hotter here in the sun every minute!"

And so, for a full hour, Dick's audience, seated under the large weeping willow on the side lawn, listened eagerly as he described the stunts he had seen; how the clowns with their red and yellow patched suits turned high somersaults to the music of the band; how the baby elephant poked his funny little snout through the bars of his cage; and how the beautiful yellow-haired lady danced on the pony's back.

Suddenly Anne burst out excitedly, "Oh, I can hardly wait!" And then quickly her smile was gone and she sat back limply, as

**REITERATION OF
STORY PROBLEM**

**EFFORTS TO
SOLVE STORY
PROBLEM**

SUSPENSE

**CONTINUED
SUSPENSE**

though she remembered something un-
pleasant.

Dick and Becky exchanged glances.

"It's Esther," Becky explained. "She was
planning to go with us, but her mother
says she's not strong enough yet. Anne's
been trying to think of some way to make
it up to her."

Dick was silent for a moment, and his
face took on a serious expression as he
dropped his head in thought. Then, glanc-
ing up as he pulled a wide blade of grass
and drew it over his lips, he said, "Maybe
sometime we can fix up a circus all our
own and put on a show just for her. Or
at least a stunt or two. Uncle Bill's dog is
learning a lot of tricks and—"

Anne drew in her breath audibly. "I
have it!"

"What?" asked Dick, a perplexed look
coming over his face.

"An imitation circus!" she exclaimed,
her yellow curls flopping with every move-
ment of her determined little head. "Yes,
sir! We've got one stunt right in our own
house! Now, Becky, don't you tell him," she
warned, as she saw that her sister understood her secret. "We'll have Dick as surprised as Esther."

Anne jumped to her feet. "Now, listen,
Dick. You go over and tell Esther she's to
come to our house as soon as she can. We've

VERB CHOICE

BEGINNING OF
CLIMAX

VERB CHOICE

got a surprise for her. Becky and I'll go on in and get things ready."

With that she started on a run for the house, Becky following close behind. A few minutes later the girls were motioning Dick and Esther to come in the side door, cautiously.

As they entered the living room and sat down, Anne tip-toed to the record player on the table and turned it on. Slow, mournful strains of an overture poured out from the record. Dick began looking around the room as though he expected something to jump out at him. Esther, a curious grin on her face, opened her mouth as though to speak. But Becky only grinned and put her fingers to her lips as a warning for both of them to keep quiet.

At the next moment their eyes lighted upon a beautiful, hand-painted screen standing in the doorway between the living room and dining room. Suddenly, and Esther blinked as though she thought her eyes were deceiving her, two small objects moved on each side of the screen. The music from the record player continued, and at last the visitors realized that the fluffy little creatures creeping into the room were kittens. Yes, Lily's three-months-old babies with their soft, spotless Angora fur.

Never did a band keep more accurate time than those four little balls of cotton as they crossed the living room floor, gin-

**SOLUTION OF
STORY PROBLEM**

VERB CHOICE

gerly lifting their tiny paws in almost perfect rhythm. Then, as the melody grew
louder, the animals crept nearer, until at
last, as the final note of the overture brought
their procession to a close, Anne squealed
with delight to see Esther's and Dick's surprised expressions.

"How's that for a circus parade?" she
asked, and at that moment the kittens scat-
tered themselves among the sofa cushions and
on to the backs of the chairs.

"Whoever heard of kittens marching to
music?" gasped Esther, her voice ending in
a squeal.

"I didn't see anything as clever as that
even in the real circus!" added Dick.

"Well, that's good," said Anne. "Maybe
Esther won't feel so bad about missing
it, now that she's seen our 'master
performance.' "

Esther's broad smile of agreement was
enough to satisfy both of the girls. "Better
yet," she added, "this didn't cost me a cent!"

"But, girls, how did you teach them
such tricks?" Dick continued.

"Well," announced Becky, "you see, we
had to get the manager's permission first."

Just then a huge, snow-white Angora
cat strutted proudly through the doorway.

"Ladies and gentlemen," Becky exclaimed, "let me present the owner of our
circus team, Lily, the mother of our musical kittens!"

Articles

The writing of juvenile articles, even for the younger readers, is also a fertile field. Naturally the scope of subject is quite limited, but once the writer sees the possibilities for this age group, he can expand at will.

In any market list you will note that the juvenile editor is always in need of the simple handicraft article, the explanation of how to make and do things; also party, game, and "rainy day" suggestions. These, then, are some of the chief things for you to go to work on, and you'll find that such articles can really be written quite easily and quickly.

But there are some very definite rules to follow in the procedure for even the simplest article. Learn from the beginning to adopt this step-by-step formula and thus assure yourself that the explanation you record on paper is as clear as that picture in your own mind or as the completed object before you.

1. Make the object yourself before you attempt to teach it to others.
2. Write the article as soon as you have finished the project so that every step is clear in your mind.
3. Have a short, inviting introduction and let the reader know at once what he can make or do.

4. Start at the very beginning and explain the procedure step by step. In the simple article, this includes the tools you work with; in more complicated ones, a separate paragraph listing materials needed is advisable because the child is less confused.

5. Write in plain, everyday language, and use short, clear-cut sentences. Always keep explanations simple.

6. Check yourself to see that no step, however easy it is for you, has been left out for the child.

7. When the article is completed, ask yourself this question: "Am I positive I could make this item by following my own directions?"

8. Any number of words is acceptable from 100 for the tiny tots to 700 for the older ones in this group. However, avoid padding or using any unnecessary words. They merely detract from the explanation and annoy the editor.

Now, then, let's analyze this simple little how-to-do according to the formula.

WRITING FOR THE TINY TOTS

SHORT
INTRODUCTION

BEGINNING

INCLUDE TOOLS
WITH EXPLAN-
ATION

IN MOST ARTICLES
THERE WOULD BE ONE
PARAGRAPH HERE IN-
STEAD OF THREE. HOW-
EVER, SINCE ALL THREE
OF THESE COLORING
METHODS HAVE BEEN USED
IN THIS PROJECT, WE
HAVE INCLUDED ALL
OF THEM.

A 225-WORD PIECE, AN
AVERAGE LENGTH HOW-TO-
DO FOR THE TINY TOTS.

Here's something the girls will enjoy making—and wearing, too. A new shiny string of beads in any color they choose.

Get a handful of pumpkin seeds and soak them thoroughly in a pan of water. Then spread them on a newspaper and let them dry in the sun. When you're sure they are completely dry, string them through the narrow end of the seed, using a sharp, coarse needle and dental floss. Make the string long enough to slip over your head, but do not fasten ends together until after the beads are colored.

To color them, you can use several different methods. Regular water colors work satisfactorily, but to make the desired color deep enough be sure that you don't have too much water on your brush.

Another way is to pour hot water over a piece of colored crepe paper and soak the seeds in this solution for several hours. The effect is a somewhat mottled bead rather than a solid color.

But to give the beads a really glossy finish, a quick-drying enamel is the best paint to use. It covers easily and provides a hard surface to the necklace, making it less likely to wear off or become chipped with use.

When the beads are dry on one side, turn the flat strand over and paint the other. When all the beads are dry, tie the ends of the string together securely.

Besides the "how-to" articles, these little folk are very often interested in bits of informative pieces—perhaps on how things are made, how things came to be invented, brief nature sketches, facts about well-known people, or even short "talks" about great historical events.

In these, too, there must be kept in mind *brevity, directness,* and a strictly *informal* style. Make your reader feel as though you were talking to him.

Things to Do

Turn to your folder of sample tiny tot magazines, read the stories therein, and list in your notebook the quality of character each contains. You will undoubtedly find on your list honesty, loyalty, kindness, and many others. You will automatically be starting to write, for the first essential is to decide what moral or character-building idea we can weave into our theme.

From these same stories, make an outline for each, following this plan:

Characters:
Time:
Place:
Plot:
    (a) Story problem
    (b) Efforts to solve problem
    (c) Climax

By continuing this practice, you will very shortly become "plot conscious," a vitally important factor because it helps us to formulate our own plots as we observe situations that would make good story material.

For writing practice, why not develop a story from the outline given on Richie and the Swiss boy? Check yourself on the results by referring to the elements of good story-writing as covered in this chapter.

Begin a daily habit of writing plot outlines and then developing them, keeping within the vocabulary and length standards for the age level.

Try a how-to article, following the formula given in this chapter. But don't let a formula keep you from being original in treatment. Your own style is what counts!

Chapter 7

WRITING FOR JUNIORS

Stories

The market for stories suitable for the junior group is greater by far than that for the tiny tots; in fact, editors seem to be ever on the lookout for them. For that reason, we attempt here to present facts that need emphasis in the writing of acceptable stories for juniors.

The 9-12's are naturally more developed than the tiny tots, are a bit more discerning, and have more diversified interests. To cope with these changes, the writer must adjust himself accordingly in handling material that is going to interest that age reader.

A. CHARACTERS

Again we say few characters in our stories, but there is definitely a *must* appearing on the horizon. Since junior magazines are still read by both boys and girls, unless you make the leading character in your story a boy, you will have only half the reader audience you intended. Girls will read, whether the main character is a boy or a girl. We wish boys weren't so fussy, but since this is absolutely a fact, don't waste time trying to figure a way out of it. Plan your story around the fellow that's going to make an appeal. Do not exclude girls from your stories, however; it is much better to have both sexes.

In the specimen story which appears a little later in this chapter you will see that we have worked for a balance of character interest. How dull the thing would be if the boys had been left out—in fact, most unnatural—for in that particular story we have a schoolroom and a school playground for our setting, and certainly both boys and girls are to be found there.

The 9-12's like to read about people their own ages, and often older, so our job is to avoid going beneath their level for our story characters. Above all, let the children in the stories solve their own problems.

B. ACTION

Observing a group of juniors in play for only a few minutes will give you plenty of ideas. One of them is bound to include activity. "Cops and robbers"—Indian forts—fire sirens—bicycle races—rodeos—exploring caves—trying to solve mysteries—these are among their favorites for playtime.

Baseball, love of pets, secrets, and the collecting fever are also an integral part of their lives. They love to entertain each other, to "steal the show," and to doll up in togs that identify them as firemen, rough cowboys, and the "cop on the beat." They thrive on competition at school. The girls love to pretend they are the teacher; and all enjoy trying something new. As always, suspense is their basis for interest.

The term *action* in a story need not necessarily mean that you must have any one of these in a wildly exciting panorama. They are mentioned here only to remind you that juniors do demand something moving, and in writing for them we must keep in mind that they do have a sense of story progress and demand a feeling that more is going to happen.

C. TITLES

As the salesman displays merchandise attractively in order that it sell, so the writer must attract his audience by a catchy display, the title. The question of naming a story or article is as important for one age level as another, but since so many other phases had to be covered in Chapter 6, we have reserved the right to wait until now to discuss it.

Human nature is the same the world over. We pass by the commonplace, ignore the uninteresting, but exclaim over the new and unusual. In a nutshell, that's the secret of good titles, too—selecting those a little unusual or with a twist one wouldn't quite expect. For instance, I referred earlier to an article of mine that appeared in a well-known writers' magazine. All I did, you see, was to change from the time-worn expression, "Variety is the spice of life," to "Variety is the Spice of Style." I also mentioned "What Time is Your English?" A little out of the ordinary, but an eye-catcher.

The new or unusual phase of a title, however, is not enough. To be a good title, it should give a hint to the reader as to what he can expect in the story or article. In other words, it should provide information. How can we hope that Johnny is going to like the cleverest story written if its title is dull, lifeless, like "Sam Brown." But change it to "Sam

Brown, the Circus Clown," and you've already suggested adventure. Naturally one doesn't want to tell
so much in the title that he arouses no curiosity.
In "Secret of the Hills" the reader does not know
what the secret is but where it is.

And then, the good title should be brief. Form
the habit of weighing titles in your mind for some
time rather than using the first one that comes to
you. The practice of alliteration (words starting with
the same letter or sound) is still good, provided the
words are meaningful and do not mislead the reader.
All of us have undoubtedly experienced reading a
book, then afterwards wondering where the author
got the title for it. It's bad business, bad enough
to pull on the adult public. Don't fool children
unless you want to kill reading interest instead of
encourage it. Perhaps one I once used, "Seeing
Through a Glass Darkly," seems a bit long but it
was taken directly from the Bible and applied to a
method of writing; therefore it would have been
meaningless had I attempted to cut it down. In
passing, too, let me say that one of the weakest
titles is that which begins with "The"; there are
exceptions, of course, where there's no way out.

D. THE BEGINNING

No longer are we living in the era of Dickens
or Scott when it was the fashion to make the reader
cover forty pages as a wind-up before the author

pitched the first ball. And what goes for the modern
novel goes for the short story as well. The string
of gayly-colored lollipops means nothing if Johnny
doesn't like the taste of the first candy. If we're
going to have our reader interested (and the editor,
too) we have to get off to a good start in the first
paragraph—better yet, in the first sentence.

If you were ten, you would not be particularly
excited about reading a story that opened this way:
"Sam and Martha had lived on the farm for twenty
years." But at ten you would be invited to read if
your eyes caught this opening sentence: "This doesn't
look too safe," Jim said as he stepped out on the
wobbly log over a rushing mountain stream. Or
perhaps this one: "It's broken!" cried Bill, staring
at the airplane model on the floor. "Tony will
never forgive me!"

E. THE ENDING

No one likes disappointment; no one likes to
be fooled. Therefore, when we are planning our
stories, let's remember that children enjoy surprises
and a satisfied feeling, too. The surprise element need
not be to the extent that the story comes out just
the opposite of what the reader thought in his own
mind would happen. But there should be a little
hint of surprise that the child had not included
in his own solution. The ending should be what
the child hopes will happen as he reads the story,

although there may be an occasion or two throughout when he thinks it isn't going to. Every youngster enjoys boasting that he "knew it would end like that." And that's nothing for the writer to steer away from in his attempt at getting suspense. One caution, though, for every beginning writer of fiction. Don't let the story drag after the climax has been reached! The thing will die on your hands very easily unless you give the child a quick, sweet-taste-in-the-mouth ending close on the heels of the big moment.

LENGTH

It is very difficult to advise a writer concerning the proper length for the simple reason that there is a rather wide variance of opinion among editors. The best guide to use, of course, is a market list (either book or magazine issue) which includes that information for the particular field and market you are interested in. In general, here is a fairly accurate scale used by many writers of juveniles.

Tiny tots (very youngest)   300-400 words
Tiny tots (in-betweens)   400-700 words
Tiny tots (7 and 8)   700-1000 words
Juniors (9-12)   1000-1800 words

Here is one of my own stories, appearing in a juvenile magazine and printed here with the publishers' permission.

Peter the Great

**INTRODUCTION OF
CHARACTERS**

**NATURALNESS OF
DIALOGUE**

**HINT AT
STORY
PROBLEM**

Peter the Great

At the bend in the road Jack halted. "Take one more look back," he said to his younger sister, "and make sure Peter isn't following us today."

Sandra turned around, swinging her dinner pail rhythmically.

"Coast's clear!" she announced. "Anyway, I guess he learned his lesson yesterday."

"Maybe," ventured her brother, a tone of doubt in his voice, at the same time casting another suspicious glance behind him. "But I wouldn't trust Pete too far. He likes to go to school too well."

"I wish he could go in my place," said Sandra as she thought of her unfinished arithmetic problems.

"Never mind. We can't have more than a hundred and sixty-five more days of it this year," Jack said. "This is the middle of the third week. Cheer up!"

Sandra laughed. "Well, if you ask me, Pete added to school instead of subtracted from it. I don't see why Miss Rennsdale—"

"Not subtracted, Sandra—distracted. She said our minds were on the cat instead of our lessons."

"Well, just because Miss Rennsdale doesn't like cats—" she muttered. Her voice trailed off to nothing, and her expression

STORY
PROBLEM

changed suddenly from a pout to a grin as she thought of their pet appearing on the school ground yesterday. He had followed close at Jack's heels every minute the gang was playing "cops and robbers" and "cowboys" and she remembered the "ah's" and "oh's" of the children when they saw him stand on his hind feet and salute the flag.

Then the bell had rung and Miss Rennsdale had announced very sharply that Jack must not let the cat come into the schoolroom. Furthermore, both he and Sandra were to see that Pete did not follow them from home again. When Jack had failed to get the cat started back up the road, Miss Rennsdale herself had used a limber switch in a fashion that made the children squirm.

"If she'd ever seen him play 'cops and robbers' with us, she wouldn't have had the heart to whip him," one girl said.

"That's right," another had agreed. "And one of these days, on some special occasion, let's make her watch him."

Several months before, with Jack's help Sandra had set out to do what no one thought could be done—teach their cat all the tricks that their cousin's dog could do. It had taken a long time, and both Jack and his sister were proud of the cat's accomplishments.

Now her eyes brightened. "If he fol-

EFFORTS TO
SOLVE THE
PROBLEM

GROWING
INTEREST

FURTHER EFFORTS
TO SOLVE THE
STORY PROBLEM

lowed us today—" but the threat of another switching loomed before them, and they entered the schoolyard quietly.

"Guess the news!" announced one of the boys as he spied Jack and Sandra coming up the walk. "Miss Rennsdale's agreed!"

"Agreed to what?" asked Jack. "What are you talking about?"

"Oh, I forgot you didn't know. Well, you see, yesterday after school two or three of us asked Miss Rennsdale why she didn't like cats. Then Fred told her all the tricks Pete could do and . . ."

"What did she say to that?" asked Sandra eagerly.

"Well, she didn't think cats were as smart as dogs."

"Ours is," snapped Sandra. "I just wish she could see him—"

"That's what I'm getting at," the boy interrupted. "Bob asked her if we could go without recesses tomorrow and then at two o'clock have a field day all our own. Fred said he'd have his dog put on a show, then we'd have you and Sandra show us all the tricks Pete can do, and we'd end up by playing cowboy so we could watch Pete's antics."

"And will she let us?" gasped Sandra, her eyes wide with excitement. "Will she let Pete come here?"

WE MUST NEVER
ENCOURAGE ANY-
THING BUT RESPECT
FOR AUTHORITY

SUSPENSE

VERB
CHOICE

"That's what she said," he announced proudly.

"I 'spect she's sorry about yesterday," Sandra said in a low voice. "She's always telling us to be kind to animals, and then—"

"Don't talk that way," scolded Jack. "You know very well that cats shouldn't be in school, and when animals don't behave, they have to be punished just as we do."

The next afternoon found a roomful of busy heads over their seat work.

Fred slipped out to go home for his dog. A few moments later a sudden clawing on the door told the children that Pete had arrived.

Sandra rose from her seat and slipped quietly to the door, carrying in her arm a small bundle. There were some curious glances at her package, but no one seemed disturbed. Miss Rennsdale, herself, seemed very much interested.

Promptly at two o'clock the group of eager spectators was seated in a semi-circle on the shady side of the playground. A large pasteboard box had been placed in front of them, the only form of "curtain" the showmen could furnish.

Fred's dog, Dance, came forward at the first whistle. Shyly he looked at his master and then, after a command from Fred, sat down and refused to budge. Twice Fred spoke to him, waiting with a hoop in his

BEGINNING
OF CLIMAX

hand for Dance to jump through. The dog seemed glued to the spot.

Fred's face turned a deep red.

"Stage fright, no doubt," said Miss Rennsdale, to help Fred out in his embarrassment.

The children giggled.

"Well, Jack, it's your turn, I guess," said Fred. "Hope your luck is better than mine."

Jack stepped forward and called Pete by his name.

"Hello, Pete," he said gently but so the audience could hear. Pete sat down and lifted his right paw.

"Oh, yes,—sure, I'll shake hands with you." The girls laughed.

"Now suppose you cross your two front paws and sit up straight." Instantly Pete took the new position.

"Now," Jack continued, as he picked the cat up in his arms, "show these people whether you like me." Pete hitched himself higher and rubbed his nose on Jack's neck.

"That's good, old boy. Now is there anyone else here that you like as well?" He put Pete down on the ground. "If there is, tell her so."

Pete walked toward the semi-circle and searched. Then, like a happy child, he hurried toward Sandra, jumped up on her lap, and repeated the performance.

**DEVELOPING
CLIMAX**

SUSPENSE

The children shouted and Miss Rennsdale smiled.

"Now, Pete," said Jack as the cat left Sandra's lap and came toward him again, "it's about time you noticed what's flying up there on the pole." Pete stopped short.

"How about a salute?" The cat sat up straight for a moment, then standing on his hind legs only, he raised his right front paw to his forehead and held it up for just an instant in salute to the flag. The crowd cheered.

"One more stunt, Pete," Jack said, "and then it's Sandra's turn. Here, Fred, will you hold one end of this rope tightly about a foot from the ground, and you, Bob, hold the other?"

Jack lifted Pete on to the rope at one end and steadied him. "All right, big boy, show them you're a tightrope walker." Pete stepped gingerly along the rope, at times barely moving more than an inch for fear he'd lose his balance.

"That's good," Jack said, as the children clapped loudly. "Now, Sandra, suppose you take over."

His sister approached the rear of the box with her bundle and sat down. Pete, following her, disappeared from sight.

In a very few minutes, Sandra stood and announced: "All of us have favorite games. Some like tag, others cops and robbers, and

SOLUTION

others hide-and-seek. But if Pete could talk, he'd name another kind." Drawing aside the box, she exclaimed proudly, "Peter, the Rootin', Tootin' Cowboy!"

There, in the full costume of a Westerner, stood Pete, braced contentedly against a small black, hand-made fence, with his big sombrero tipped over one ear—surveying his audience with joy and pride!

Squeals and shouts greeted him.

"We think that's a pretty neat trick, Miss Rennsdale. What do you call it?" Jack asked.

Miss Rennsdale burst out laughing. "You win!" she said. "If I were you, I'd call him Peter the Great!"

Articles

Since this junior group is identified by its abundance of activity and eagerness to be doing something, here again is the writer's chance to take inventory and fill the need. The junior is as much a "parrot" as the tiny tot. If friend Tom can make a kite, it is well for Jack to try it, too. If Betsy has decided to adopt a hobby of collecting salt and pepper shakers like Aunt Susan's, then she will be very likely to interest her playmates in some similar enterprise. So if the "do as I do" or the "see what fun it is" element is such a vital part of their lives, we can still rely on two types of articles mentioned earlier, the how-to-do and the how-to-make.

In addition to these, the juniors are ready to accept informative articles provided they are developed in a sweet-toothed style rather than as a bookish reading assignment and provided, too, that those articles are not too long.

1. HOW-TO-MAKE

The "how-to-make" article can be considerably more complicated than that prepared for the tiny tot. The tools 9-12's are familiar with, their capacity for constructing things from directions, and their eagerness to try something new so they can teach or show it to their friends all indicate a marked advancement over the little ones. Such being the case, the "how-to-make" article often follows some scheme of presentation like this:

  a. A list of materials needed
  b. An inviting introduction to the project
  c. Explanation of procedure
  d. Photo accompanying article (Not always necessary. The subject of illustration is discussed later.)

Dwelling of the Dwarfs which I sold to a junior level magazine is an example of this type of article. Analyze it according to the formula.

Dwelling of the Dwarfs

What You'll Need

  1 pasteboard carton 12"x18"x24"
  1 pasteboard carton half as large
  White wrapping paper to cover both
  Red paper, as heavy as you can find
  Artificial snow and cotton batting
  2 large Mother's Oats boxes
  5 of the next size
  String of Christmas tree lights
  Scissors, paste, roping

INTRODUCTION TO SUBJECT

INVITATION TO MAKE PROJECT

BEGINNING OF CONSTRUCTION

What story of strange little people has become any more of a favorite than "Snow-White and the Seven Dwarfs"? Everyone, it seems, from tiny brother to great-grandma, is acquainted with the experiences of Dopey, Bashful, and their five little brothers.

But had you ever thought that you could see the kind of castle those busy little dwarfs lived in, the kind all glisteny with snow on the outside and with its beautiful colored lights streaming through the windows and from its magic walls?

Well, the fun of building that very castle can be yours with only a few necessary bits of material, and by following the directions carefully, you will be surprised how soon you can have an attractive display for some "showy corner" in your home or schoolroom. It could even be used as an appropriate feature for a Christmas window scene. So get busy at collecting a few odds and ends, and if you prefer, call in a playmate or two to work with you and share the fun.

After you have finished your "collecting spree" of the materials suggested at the beginning, you are ready to construct the main floor of the castle. Draw a crescent-shaped (half moon) piece in center of front about 8 inches from the bottom of the largest box and cut out with knife. Below this, leaving an inch of solid cardboard, cut a

**PROGRESSIVE
EXPLANATION**

EXPLANATION OF UNFAMILIAR TERMS

doorway of same width as crescent. Cut in half the cardboard which you just removed and fasten each side to the inside of the box with adhesive tape so that the doors will swing when "off to work they go."

On either side of the castle cut out one arched window, leaving back side without any opening. Now you are ready to cover the entire surface of the larger box, even the top. See that the surface is pasted smoothly so that you can be sure of four neat walls. Cut strips of paper the same length as each side dimension of the box and two inches wide. Notch each strip every other inch two inches deep. By pasting this strip on the edge of the box so that it stands erect, we have a feature common to all old castles.

Now for the two front turrets (towers). Using the two large-sized Mother's Oats boxes, cut out two windows and cover surface with white paper. Instead of using its original cover place a red conical-shaped roof on each. Roof is made from cutting a triangle out of a large red circle and pasting the sides together. Cut out a rectangular piece from rear of turret and attach turret to the two front corners of the box with adhesive tape. The two rear turrets, made of smaller Mother's Oats boxes, are placed about one-third the distance from the top of the box to the floor.

The second story of the castle is made

ALWAYS MAKE CLEAR
WHAT PART CHILD IS WORKING ON

KEEP UP THE READER'S INTEREST
IN FINAL RESULTS

ANY 800-WORD
PIECE, AVERAGE
LENGTH FOR
JUNIORS

exactly like the first only for the openings. One arched doorway on the front and one on either side is all that is necessary before the outside covering is pasted on. Fasten the notched edging, two front turrets at bottom level, and one rear turret very high.

And now for the showy part! Apply paste to the outside of the entire castle, roofs and all, a small portion at a time, and while the paste is still moist, sprinkle artificial snow on the surface. Cut out two tiny wreaths of dark green paper and paste on the swinging doors.

Spread cotton batting (or some crumpled white crepe paper if it's easier to get) on a good-sized table and sprinkle that with artificial snow, too. Green Christmas roping adds just the right touch for the base of the castle and also to form a front yard hedge effect. Any tiny sprigs of evergreen or little artificial trees on standards can easily be arranged to complete the setting. Place a string of Christmas tree lights inside the castle and watch the variety of colors streaming through the windows and out on to the sparkling snow all around.

The little dwarfs, yes, all seven of them, can be purchased in almost any five and ten cent store for a small amount. So with the little men out in the front guarding the scene, it's time to call in your friends and show them the delightful little castle with its seven towers.

2. HOW-TO-DO

The "how-to-do" fits equally well into the activity of this age level, for the junior finds group contests, parties, and neighborhood projects just as delightful as his individual challenge of skill.

Here we have an example of a "how-to-do" that always makes an appeal to 9-12's, that of learning a new game. Again, the job of the writer is to work for simplicity and clarity. He must understand thoroughly what he wants others to learn.

Word Whiz

Here's a game you will enjoy playing, and the next time you have some of your friends in, we will wager that they, too, will work like beavers to see who can fill in all the blanks first.

But don't stop there. After you have worked out this one, make up a chart all your own and ask dad or mother to compete with you.

G   R   A   S   P

Country
Animal
Flower
City
Food

You will see at the top of the chart the word GRASP. To the left we have a list of various items: country, animal, flower, etc. For each letter in the word GRASP see if you can name a country that begins with that letter; then an animal, flower, etc. When you have finished, you will have filled in 25 words. Be sure you have not named a city for a country, nor an insect for an animal.

Remember that many different cities, food, and other things begin with the same letter, but the object of the game is not to write any particular ones in, but to see who in the group can get all 25 blanks filled in first correctly.

Your fun doesn't end here. You can work for a wide variety of names by changing any of the five items at the left. For example, substitute for country the word bird; change some of the others to fruit, author, fish, automobile, river, or vegetable.

The key word at the top should have at least five letters in it, as GRASP does, but it can have more than one vowel. Try using such words as leans, snare, trods, drown, flows, bread, and grand. You will have fun surprising yourself for a long, long time, for by changing the key word or a few of the items each time, you will soon discover that two games are never alike.

Country	Germany	Russia	Asia	Spain	Portugal
Animal	goat	reindeer	ape	skunk	porcupine
Flower	geranium	rose	aster	snap-dragon	pansy
City	Glasgow	Roanoke	Akron	Spokane	Pasadena
Food	grapes	raisins	apricots	steak	parsnips

Your answer may look something like this.

3. THE INFORMATIVE ARTICLE

To capture the reader's interest is, of course, step one in writing the successful juvenile article. Think of that beginning sentence as you would of a pebble cast into the smooth surface of a brook. Let a ripple of interest penetrate the child's mind.

That done, you are ready to proceed. Now because an article is written chiefly for its information, the beginning writer often concentrates on a progressive presentation of facts. This type of writing will do nothing but kill the child's interest in reading further. Instead, your aim should be to write as you would talk. Imagine your reader to be in actual conversation with you, for the conversational style is the only one that assures you that your audience can assimilate what you are handing out.

Use the second person as much as possible. Your reader likes to feel that you had him personally in mind when you prepared your article. Give him the honest impression that you are writing for him because you are concerned about him and his knowledge of your subject.

Don't be afraid of an occasional question. It promotes attention.

Above all, explain as you tell and explain as clearly as possible. Remember that your reader knows much less about the subject than you do. You have made a study of it; examine that subject from every possible angle. Be specific, with a sincere matter-of-factness about you.

Don't write down to your readers and don't write up to them. Don't be afraid of an occasional big word. Its use often gratifies their vanity and, anyhow, youngsters can often guess its meaning by the way it appears in context. Put yourself on a level with them. If you don't, your article will fall upon barren ground. Even juniors demand that what they read be neither childish nor too obscure for their years!

Here is an example of a junior informative. Note the conversational tone as well as the other qualities mentioned in this discussion.

Lord of the Land Down Under

It is noon, and you have just stepped out on to a barren mass of ice and snow in the far Antarctic. The temperature is seventy degrees below zero. You shudder as you look about and think of the expeditions that have been made to this far-away land. You suddenly realize what Admiral Byrd and others have experienced here—exposure, loneliness, danger. You gaze out from your numerous pounds of furs inpatiently. After all, you came here on a mission all your own—to see that sophisticated little man that lives in this far South.

A sound of chatter attracts your attention. There, marching down the glassy ocean edge in long, regular lines, comes a file of soldiers in their black and white military array. Their short, flipper-like wings look like arms from a distance; their large, webbed feet paddle awkwardly along as they seem to travel in rhythm. As they come closer, though, you lose the idea of a marching regiment. Instead, each one looks like a fat little man in an evening suit, with a shiny white front, and black back and shoulders. You decide the man was right who called the penguin a "strutting senator."

The bitter sub-zero air may bite at your face, but this stout little fellow doesn't mind the cold. His feathers secrete an oil which gives him protection. Besides, a heavy layer of fat underneath his skin keeps him warm.

The group moves on past you and heads for the water's edge. Like human beings, they have decided it's time for a little recreation. Approaching the water, they set up a loud chatter and soon you discover that the object of every bird in that little group is to get one of the others to go into the water first.

Pushing, dodging the other fellow's blows, they resemble a group of boys and girls about to dive into a swimming hole. Occasionally one does get pushed in, but with a bound he's back on the ice again, eager now for revenge. Then suddenly one of them starts running full speed along the ice, the rest following close at his heels.

A quick dive into the water means "follow the leader," each one taking off from exactly the same spot as the first. Several minutes of silence follow; then coming to the surface about twenty-five yards from the edge, they engage in a rolling and splashing exercise, cleaning themselves and uttering yells at each other. A few of them, playing truant for a while, ride on moving ice floes before joining the others on shore.

It's time now to eat, and that means the sea birds must take their turns chasing silvery little sardines and herrings. Unless the penguin catches the fish in just the right fashion, he's due for a very sore throat from trying to swallow it. The only successful way is to catch it in the middle, give it a quick twist, and swallow it head first. In that way the sharp edge of the gill covers and the scales point backward. Being deft swimmers and deep divers, they have little difficulty in satisfying their appetites.

Peace-loving birds, the penguins prove themselves quite affectionate toward one another. The only time, in fact, when jealousy seems to creep into their midst is in mating season. Their nests are built on bare rock, using small pebbles and sometimes grass and leaves. Frequently some thieving penguin steals pebbles from another nest to use for his own and then guiltily sneaks away. But if seen in the act by the owner, he will never try to get any more; he's too busy getting away from the bird in pursuit.

The penguin's eggs, usually two, are about four inches long and three inches in diameter. After the young are hatched, both parent birds care for and feed the young, their main concern being protection against sea gulls and hooligan cocks.

There are about fifteen kinds of penguins, and the

birds are very numerous where they are found. Though the Antarctic region claims most of them, a few have been found as far north as New Zealand and Brazil. The common penguin stands about two and a half feet tall and weighs seventy-five pounds. They are poor runners because their legs are short and very far back on their bodies. They act much like boys and girls in their ideas of fun, whether it is a game of tag or a "free ride" on a cake of ice. And they even seem to tattle on one another just as you're very likely to do sometimes.

Here they come, strutting up the icy edge again, and chattering away loudly. Who knows? Maybe they are talking about you now!

Things to Do

Again we suggest that you turn to your files of magazines and papers for the 9-12's and study the stories published. Make plot analysis outlines for several of them. Note particularly, too, the verb choice, ways of injecting description, and naturalness of dialogue they contain.

For your own writing practice, use these simple facts from which to build an outline and develop a story.

A. Sam attempts to teach John how to ski. Three miles from home, a severe snow storm comes up. Sam, afraid John will think him a quitter, continues the sport. In a blinding mass of snow John is injured. Broken ski and sprained ankle necessitate

Sam's dragging him to a cabin. The storm continues to rage and Sam decides they are going to need more help. On his way for rescuers, Sam crashes into a half-buried sleigh. Woodsmen hear his cries, listen to his story, and rescue John from the isolated hut. Sam's bravery wins a lasting approval from John.

B. Cynthia and her friend Donna attend the county fair. Mother and dad have made arrangements for the girls to return home with a neighbor later. At the appointed time, the girls arrive at the booth where the neighbor is to meet them. He is not there. Donna is panic stricken; Cynthia thinks hard how to handle the situation. A vain search of the grounds and a series of fruitless inquiries help Cynthia to decide on a plan. Both girls race to the "doughnut booth" and ask to earn money for car fare home. The kind woman sees their predicament, hires them for an hour, and supplies them with a bag of doughnuts to eat on the way. They arrive home just as Cynthia's father is driving out of the garage on his way back to the fair for them.

In each case refer to the "test" questions in an earlier chapter as a check on your story.

Chapter 8

WRITING FOR
THE INTERMEDIATES

Stories

We have now reached the age level when we no longer talk about writing for boys and girls; it's a matter of writing for boys or girls. Not every publishing company has separate magazines for each; but because many do, it is an issue we must keep in mind when we decide to slant our material.

True, if we have selected a special Sunday School paper designed for both sexes to which we would like to submit a story, our job is to write a story that has appeal to both. Naturally, to meet that need, the writer must combine the two sexes in his story.

We do not imply that boys' magazines carry stories with boy characters only, nor that girls' stories limit themselves to girl characters. What we should imply, though, is that a story slanted for a girls' paper should have a girl for a leading character; for boys, a story with a male leading character.

It is needless to say that the 12-15's interests are far more diversified than those of the two younger groups. This fact is, obviously, the basis for editors publishing separate magazines.

A. SUBJECTS

As the result of careful questioning, examining periodicals that are popular with this age group, observing the interests of the 12-15's, and relying upon hundreds of statements they have written themselves, we list here several subjects that seem to have the strongest appeal to these young people, not necessarily shown in order of interest.

1. For boys:

    (a) Sports   (They are ardent fans of baseball, football, basketball, racing)

    (b) Contests   (Stress is on sportsmanship and team work more than simple physical activity)

    (c) Camping   (This includes hiking, swimming, diving, and other activities popular with perhaps the Scout program)

    (d) Fishing; hunting; skiing

(e) Outdoor   adventures   (Cave   explorations, cabin construction,
club   work)

(f) Aviation

(g) Radio

(h) Invention

(i) Science

(j) Animals   (They   love   dog   and
horse stories)

(k) Sea stories

(l) Historical tales   (especially westerns)

(m) Mystery

2. For girls:

(a) Sports

(b) Domestic   (Home stories)

(c) School

(d) Career   (Vocational because young
people like to earn money;
sometimes fictionalized biography)

(e) Humor

(f) Historical tales

(g) Other lands

(h) Vacation

(i) Hobbies   (Stamp, shell, coin collection, etc.)

(j) Mystery

B. PLOT

The older the child, the more complicated the plot of a story can be. However, the basic story problem, efforts to solve that problem, and climax remain the skeleton on which to hang the details of every story. And as we have stressed previously, the solution must be made by the characters themselves.

So often we forget that the word *juvenile* covers anything beyond the ten-year-old. As a result, the old tendency (and a fatal one) is that of writing down to them. Nothing can help us cut our throats any more readily. When we make it our job to understand our reader and his world, our writing will take on a warmth that will make them respond favorably to what we have to say.

The 12-15-year-old has many of the same experiences her seniors have. She is interested in solving school problems, vocational problems, and boy problems. She rebels against boredom; she seeks sympathy and help; she admires strength of personality and wit in others; she loves suspense, activity, and the chance to read herself into the story you write for her.

In developing the plot, we must see to it that the story unfolds gracefully before our eyes, that is, like a series of scenes taking place on a stage. With that thought in mind, we will be less likely to allow blackouts. These are the occasions we take to describe, present facts, or tell about our characters. Beware of blackouts! Rather than "tell about" let the reader watch the stage himself and get the story first-hand through dialogue and action.

C. PLOT ANALYSIS

Perhaps the hardest question for the beginning writer to face is this: "Would the theme for a story that I have in mind for them really appeal to the 12-15's? Or is it too childish, or too sophisticated?"

I believe the easiest way to help others determine the answer is by illustration. Rather than study one story as a specimen this time, we cite here several nut-shell stories that have appeared in intermediate story papers. They should serve as a means of comparison between themes you may select for development and those which are and have been acceptable. In addition to these, the sample papers you have in your files will furnish a comparative study.

Story One

A young girl from Holland is introduced to a group of young people at a club party. Her simplicity and demure smile win friends for her at once, among them Ted Powers. But somehow, from time to time that evening, those in the group notice an expression of sadness, almost weakness on the girl's part. Through a chance remark made by one of the boys about a news broadcast at the dinner hour, the girl's eyes suddenly fill with tears. Ted, ever alert, uses his customary diplomacy in learning the secret. By his cleverness, the young people get Kathleen's story, a heart-breaking one of the deplorable conditions she has left behind when she came to this country to live with an aunt and uncle. An immediate response from the group comes, and activity begins. As a project for their club, they organize a "teen-age booster corps" to raise money for Kathleen's invalid father so that he, too, can come and live in this country their new friend has already learned to love.

Story Two

Lola Winters is very much disturbed at seeing Bill James, a newcomer in high school, cheating in an exam by reading from Helen's paper. Her first impulse is to tattle, but quickly decides against it. If Helen were aware of it, maybe it was done to attract him as a friend. In the cafeteria that noon she is again taken aback to see Helen, Bill, and Helen's twin brother eating together. Spying Lola, the three ask her to join them.

She accepts somewhat hesitantly, but Bill is so much the gentleman that she finds herself strangely drawn into his company. When school is dismissed that afternoon, Bill asks Lola to meet him in the classroom where the examination had taken place; the grades, he understands, have been posted. Anxious to see if Bill's and Helen's are the same, Lola is in for another surprise. Bill's mark is 90; Helen's, 40; Lola's, 80. When Lola learns that Bill has been watching Helen take the examinations now for two weeks and has noticed that her eyes are so bad she can't see the blackboard questions, a sense of guilt at misjudging him sweeps over her. To climax her surprise, he tells her that he and Bill are sending their "walk-shoveling money" to the clinic so that Helen can have glasses. It doesn't take long for Lola to see what Bill is really made of and why she has found herself drawn to him.

Story Three

Hank wishes above all else to make the high school football team. The one thing that is likely to prevent him is his math mark. With exams around the corner, he finds himself rather despondent. Bill and Jim, both splendid players, approach Hank and confide in him a secret. If he wants to make the team as badly as they want him to, he can do it. They have the solution. Bill has found a poorly mimeographed copy of the test in the teacher's waste basket and is willing to share it with Hank. Much as football appeals to him, he refuses to be dishonest. In hot anger, Bill and Jim walk away. When the exam is taken, the two fellows discover that the test has been changed. Both fail it and Hank passes. They immediately accuse Hank of squealing on them. As he takes his place on the field the following Saturday, he is met with jeers and taunts. Once in the game, his mind is in chaos, and at the half the coach reprimands him and all the players severely for being dead on their feet. He asks if they are trying to do a job on Hank, and one reveals that they don't like squealers. As soon as the game is resumed, the coach seeks out Bill and Jim to get the story. Having pried the truth out of them, he goes to the math teacher who clears Hank at once by saying that he discovered one of the poor copies in the hall and knew some must be in circulation so had changed the test. Between quarters, the coach reveals the true story to Hank. Relieved, he goes back into the game and fights bitterly and brilliantly. The showing he makes for the team is not soon forgotten by the school and he accepts apologies from Bill, Jim, and the other players.

D. PROPER INGREDIENTS FOR THE STORY

(1) **Sound characterization** Unless alive and natural for the role he takes, whether it be hero, clown, or cowboy, the character can determine the strength or weakness of the plot. Keep always before you the question: Is this character a believable one? Would he act this way in real life?

(2) **Fresh Angle in Plotting** The easiest mistake for a beginning writer to make is that of choosing a time-worn plot. If, in some cases, an old plot is used, there must very definitely be a fresh handling of it.

(3) **Realism** The writer must not kid himself into thinking that because he's writing for juveniles, he must include only the bright, goody-goody side of life, the side from which he hopes his reader will derive a wholesome lesson. On the contrary, the 12-15 is already very much aware of what the world is like, even though he may not personally have participated in it. He has been around long enough now to have observed that the hero in life doesn't always get the recognition he deserves; that the fellow he's rooting for in the race frequently comes in behind the winner; that sacrifice doesn't always bring material reward; that it takes far more courage to say "no" than "yes"; and that the strongest

fellow in the world is the chap who can resist temptations.

And may we add, the average editor does like real, honest-to-goodness boys who can meet tests of courage and who aren't afraid to fight for the right. You see, the wholesome lesson you were trying to get across may be in the story but not, we hope, by giving the reader a sissy to ridicule. Don't ever be guilty of receiving a rejection slip on the grounds that "life situations aren't like those in your story." We are not advocating stark realism, but at least enough of it to mirror everyday happenings.

E. SETTING

(1) The safest bet is sticking to activities 12-15's are familiar with; that is, locating your story where the reader can picture himself easily—the baseball diamond, the school gymnasium, the swimming pool, the park, the hunting trip, the abandoned shack, his uncle's cabin, etc.

(2) The unusual setting, wherein one can teach his reader authentic facts while telling an interesting story. And the average 12-15-year-old enjoys having woven into his story facts about such things as the lobster industry, dog teams of the far North, the romantic West, etc.

F. BEGINNINGS

We have pointed out that the first requisite of our plot is a story problem. For the very young reader that problem should appear early in the story, even in the first sentence if one wishes.

We have not, up to this point, mentioned the various ways of plunging into our story. Briefly, the beginning of every story should place emphasis on one of these three: a) action, (b) character, or (c) dialogue. Whichever you choose, remember this rule: the beginning sets the mood for the story. Remember, too, that the opening lines of a story are its shop window. If it's a sports story, then start with sports, not a picnic.

It is up to the writer to determine the type of story he is writing; then his job is to determine whether the beginning he has chosen does depict the mood of the story or present the type of character he has in mind.

Often the beginnings are the very hardest part of story-writing to master. It is not unusual to find beginners trying as many as a dozen times, even without success, and then coming back after the story is completed to re-work the opening paragraph.

G. ENDINGS

Personally I have found that endings give students more trouble than beginnings. And there is no phase of writing more difficult to explain. By this time you have seen that there is a plot formula to follow; that there are very definite ways of revealing character so that they will come alive and stay alive for us; that dialogue itself can be patterned; yes, that even the beginning can be written after an established model. But when we come to the ending, it so much depends on all that has been involved in the story—characters, dialogue, problems, suspense—that we can simply say: It must coincide with all the rest.

Some writers, after plotting their story, work on the ending first. Others prefer to start their stories and allow the characters to work out their own endings. Whichever method is used, our safest bet in determining the quality of an ending is to test it with these questions:

(a) Is it logical?

(b) Does it ring true with the details that preceded it?

(c) Does it remain consistent with the character?

(d) Does it satisfy the reader in every respect?

H. LENGTH

The average story length for intermediates runs about 2200 words; however, the needs of the individual editors are indicated in the regular market lists published in writers' magazines and handbooks. One should consult either of these as he prepares to slant his material.

I. TABOOS

The writer, to sell his story, must be aware that there are certain features which editors refuse to accept in stories, especially those appearing in religious publications. Among these are profanity, drinking, smoking, gambling, card playing, dancing, the theater, crime, kidnapping, warfare, guns, or an inkling of propaganda. Equally undesirable are tacked-on morals, class or race distinction, underprivileged boys and girls, emphasis on luck, belittling of police, poor grammar, and moss-grown plots.

Articles

The article should be our special concern when we are dealing with the 12-year-olds and up. Earlier we studied the simple how-to-do, how-to-make, and the simple informative articles.

Now let's see what is happening in the article field for the older juveniles. Here, it would appear, are fertile acres for the writer to dig his heels into, and by a careful, thorough study, prepare himself for the reaping of a harvest that from all appearances is going to have a steady market for years to come.

First of all, we must concede the fact that everyone seems to be reading articles, and everyone includes the early teen-agers! There is no more forceful an influence for years toward making the "article habit" a household custom than is that which has been exerted by *Reader's Digest*. Together with its contemporaries, we have seen the germ grow until it has spread into both religious story papers and secular juvenile magazines. For a further eye-opener, take a glance at the contents of such magazines as *Seventeen, Calling All Girls, Boy's Life, American Girl,* as well as dozens of Sunday School publications, and notice the percentage of articles compared with fiction in each issue.

The answer is obvious: One should start at the beginning, give diligent study and practice to this fascinating job of article writing, and master it!

Out of the many, many types of articles suitable for this age group, we have room here for only three. The world over, we always find those who enjoy a deep interest in the scenic spots that have been provided for us. Whether it's the study of color phenomena, mystical depths of the great caverns, or some pinnacle of beauty erected by man, youth agrees with the poet Wordsworth when he said,

"Earth has not anything to show more fair;
Dull would he be of soul who could pass by
A sight so touching in its majesty."

And so, for our first study, let us consider

THE NATURE ARTICLE

We shall select for our subject one of Florida's most beautiful shrines, the famous Singing Tower. Since the idea of a tower's singing is rather unusual, even though the name is commonplace to many, we'll use it for our title.

Now the first paragraph of any article must serve a dual purpose. It must catch the reader's interest and also lead to the core of the article. In other words, the reader must know by the end of the first paragraph a few of the five W's: who, what, where, when, and why; not as directly or emphatically, of course, as in a standard newspaper report but at least enough so the reader will know where he's going.

The introduction can take one of three forms: (a) the question method, (b) the exclamatory method or (c) statement of fact. The latter must often be of a fictional nature to captivate the reader's attention.

Let's use the fictional method for our beginning and see what we can do with it.

The Singing Tower

Slowly he took the last few steps to the summit and turned his face toward the West. He drew in his breath quickly. Then, surveying the view in a panoramic fashion, his eyes filled with a mist and he reached for his hat reverently. Never had he seen such a ruby red mingling with amber green to make a western sky. Never had the deep valleys below seemed so much like hallowed ground. Here on the very top of the mountainside, Edward Bok's soul was being stirred by the hand of God.

In this first paragraph, you will see that we have where (a summit); when (sunset); who (Edward Bok). Besides, we have included action and an appeal to the sense of sight.

A bit of dialogue is good in any article, but since Edward Bok is alone on a summit, we shall alter it a bit by having him muse to himself as he views the scene below.

"It's like a dream," he muttered as he braced himself against a tree and gazed out over the wide expanse before him. "Truly a wonderland up here." But the sound of his own voice marred the sanctity of the place for him, and he leaned forward, his eyes intent again upon the sky. Long minutes he stood there until he sensed his eyes were fairly piercing the fast approaching dusk of the evening. Somehow, the calmness that had come with it had brought to him, too, a feeling of peace, and in a moment he sat down, relaxed, in the strange stillness. He watched the Florida moon rise above the deep green forests of pine, and for the first time in his life Iron Mountain took on a new meaning.

Now in order to show the why of the story—that is, to let the reader know just enough of Bok's background to see the significance of his response to this incident, we use a bit of flashback and more dialogue.

Edward Bok's mind went back to the days when he was a young man in Holland. There had been self-denials, hardships, back there. The struggle against odds to maintain a family had driven his parents to America when he was only six. But with him he had brought the memory of some words his grandfather had spoken as the boy had taken leave of the old man.

"Make the world a bit more beautiful or better, my lad, because you have been in it," he had said. And tonight as Edward Bok looked out over the scene from the mountain top, those words stood before him as though painted in a lighted sign across the sky. "Make it more beautiful than this?" he asked himself. "How could I?"

Again Bok's thoughts raced back to the time when old Netherlands was being infested with pirates. His grandfather, he recalled, had been given a barren island to guard and had been warned that no armed vessels should land. The task had had its responsibilities, but for his grandfather the work was not enough, and soon the old man had set about planting trees, shrubs, and berries as a refuge for the birds of the stormy seas. It had been crudely planned, perhaps, but it had served its purpose, a sanctuary.

Arriving at the word sanctuary, we have now hit upon the what. And incidentally, the transition from fictional style to factual is taking place. From this point on, we have the how, and it is obvious that the facts contained in the remainder of the article are the result of research. But more about research after you have finished reading it.

And so, in 1928 the work of Florida's magnificent Singing Tower was begun. No material was too costly, no efforts too great to go into the construction of this beauty spot of the Southland. The base of the tower was made of coquina rock, a soft, whitish limestone made of broken shells and corals extracted from the National Gardens near Daytona, Florida. Pink and gray marble was brought from Europe for its construction.

Carved on the pinnacles of the tower today are figures of birds, animals, and plants of that region. On the entrance door, inscribed in hammered brass, are twenty-six pictures depicting the story of the Creation as revealed in Genesis. Seventy-one bells, some of the finest ever cast in England, hang at the top of the tower. The largest one, the Bourdon, weighs over eleven tons.

For several years now since the completion of this beautiful piece of architecture, the Singing Tower, two hundred fifty feet high, has stood in the midst of Florida's picturesque sanctuary at Mountain Lake. Over a hundred varieties of birds, both native and migrant, have been identified in this region.

The tower itself is surrounded by a moat intended to keep the general public out. Stately palm trees line the pool in front, giving it a perfect setting. Only the mellow pealing of the great bells which ring out all day and night, as well as the birds that choose to live there, unmolested, now guard Edward Bok's body which lies in a crypt near the north door of the tower.

Edward Bok, the man who had started on a 50¢ a week job in a bakery shop and had steadily climbed to the position of

author, editor, and sponsor of the American
Peace Award, had found one more way to
give something back to the people who had
shared with him the America he had dreamed
about.

A WORD ABOUT RESEARCH

The word research needs more than passing mention. One doesn't write a story or article for juveniles
merely by relating an incident and adorning it with
frills or explaining some fact without support for the
statements made. In both one must be accurate in
presenting details so that the child will never have
erroneous impressions left with him. To be sure that
his reader has the true conception of place, weather
conditions, term, custom, or whatever the story contains, the writer's job must be to read before he
writes! Thus research, even in the writing of fiction,
is a "key to the craft."

The method of note-taking, whether on 3x5 cards,
scratch pad, or notebook paper, is of minor conse-
quence. The important thing is to provide yourself
with more facts than you really need. The beginning
writer is likely to regard this advice as "bunk," main-
taining that if he isn't going to use all the notes he
took, why the extra exertion? They forget that the
people that mail the pay checks for writing are experienced at judging a piece and can readily detect
whether the author had to squeeze hard every word
in his notes to round out that 1000-worder he'd been

aiming at, or whether by careful analysis of facts and culling of the irrelevant notes, he has left an article that is meaty and appealing. Besides, the more notes one takes on a subject, the better over-all picture he has of that subject, the notes aiding him in organizing his material.

THE INSPIRATIONAL ARTICLE

A second type of article unusually adaptable to this age level is the inspirational one, sometimes in editorial form, sometimes in a fictional sketch with an application made at the end.

Remember that the 12-15's are in the process of making adjustments socially, physically, and often spiritually. The books they read, the friends they make, the experiences they have at school, the responsibilities they are given at home all tend to influence their thinking and consequently their conduct. If, then, the writer can take advantage of this malleable state and can produce articles that will furnish idealistic thinking, challenging facts, and an appeal to their better selves, he is rendering a vital service. He will, incidentally, be encouraging youth to look for an interest in the things that are lasting.

Following the fictional sketch pattern, we have here "Christ of the Andes," referred to in an earlier chapter. Since our aim is to inspire, we must not only make our subject a vital one but we must show that it is a current one. In other words, no matter how antiquated the theme, it must have bearing on present day thinking and living, or the reader is going to say, "Let the past die."

Christ of the Andes

High up in the Andes Mountains stands a statue, situated on the boundary between Argentina and Chile. At its feet are engraved these words: "Sooner shall these mountains crumble into dust than Argentines and Chileans break the peace sworn at the feet of Christ the Redeemer."

Notice how quickly after the factual introductory paragraph we make mention of its meaning for us today. To further the emphasis we use present tense.

The circumstances by which the statue came to be erected is not a singular one, but what its presence on the mountain top reveals today is most significant.

Now, in order to get the story told, we must slip to past tense and review the facts. To hasten over the general situation, we use a series of clauses, most effective method of saving time.

At the turn of the century, the story goes, diplomatic relations between the countries had reached their limit. Warships were in readiness; men had been called from the fields and their homes to come into the forts and be drilled into armies; rich and poor were asked to pay for these things. The spring of 1900 found a conflict about to begin.

It is time for the touch of dialogue as we introduce the main character, the originator of the idea, and the second character in the following paragraph.

Then Easter Sunday dawned. With new hope and conviction an old bishop of the Argentine Republic faced his congregation. "Why build warships?" he asked. "Why drill armies? Why not be friends with neighbors?" He urged them to stop and reflect; reminded them that war never proved who was right— it only showed whose army was the strongest, whose strategy was best. And then, in the spirit of humility of the Master Himself, he urged them to remember the teachings of Christ.

News of that message was carried over the mountains. Bishop Java urged his people, too, to work for peace, not war. But hostile relations did not cease with a mere request from two religious leaders. It took weeks, yes, months for a revolution of opinion to come about. The boundary line, over which the dispute had started in the first place, was still an argumented issue.

Again, the short, factual review of events.

> There followed hours of study; opinions of neutral countries were sought; finally a settlement satisfactory to both sides was reached. But it was more than the settlement of mere boundary. The paper those two countries endorsed was a Treaty of Arbitration, one of the first in the world, in which it was agreed that all questions should be settled peacefully.

To give the piece a touch of drama is the aim of the next paragraph.

> Such was the hope of an Argentine bishop. And such was the vision of the man who later was privileged to witness one of the most unusual ceremonies history has ever recorded. In 1904, there in the Andes, came men, women, and children to spend the night on the mountain. The people of the Argentine camped on the Chilean side; the people of Chile, on that of the Argentines to show that they were friends. There was a great sound of music; shouts and songs echoed across the valleys. And the next afternoon at sunset, when the statue was unveiled, the people beheld in the last glow of the sun, a bronze figure of Christ, made from the metal of old guns. Silently the people knelt and prayed that the whole world might be

at peace as they were. It was as though they
had heard the command:

> "Fling down your swords;
> Be friends again;
> You are not wolf-packs—
> You are men!"

Now we have reached the place for personal application. Note the editorial "we" is employed from this
point on. This practice is a *must*, for as surely as we
use "you" instead of "we," we are literally pointing
our fingers to the reader and preaching.

The secret of that peace established better than a half century ago lies in one word:
understanding. True today, as then, it must
be common among all men if we are to proceed in the building of a world where peace
shall prevail. But our problem is even a
more serious one; it has reached international
dimensions.

One of our ambassadors once said, "It is
my conviction that a world of peace involves
more than the good intentions of one democracy to keep it safe from outside peril. It is
only when a determined majority of the
people, in whose name the United Nations
Charter was written, share their faith in this
great cause, that the most important factor
for success has been realized." Faith, then, in
the cause of peace, is our first obligation.

Only then can we wield influence for peace over other peoples of the world.

But no nation, not even America, can be strong in its influence over others if it deliberately and willfully allows its own borders to be tainted with corruption. Our job is to strive for an understanding among ourselves, to maintain peaceful relations between labor and industry, to embrace a more rigid code of ethics in the business of life.

In our own strength all this is impossible, but with the same spirit that prompted the South American republics to swear their peace at the feet of the Redeemer, we can accomplish the task. Yes, we, too, need the Christ of the Andes.

THE PROFILE

A third type with popular appeal to the early teen-agers is the personality sketch or profile, dealing with a person who has done something really important or who is versatile in his accomplishments.

Actually this type can be inspirational to youth, for it not only instructs but sets an example. Our aim, of course, should be to select someone whose life has a message. But at the same time, we must guard against personalities that are overly familiar through history—generals, statesmen, Presidents. Even names like Florence Nightingale, Joan of Arc, Henry Ford, though excellent subjects in themselves, sometimes get a cold shoulder because they have been so much written about.

People in the field of science, art, sculpture, teaching, writing, medicine and many others are simply waiting to be used as subjects. By all means, though, the articles must not be textbookish. If they are, one might better save his postage than to impose upon the good graces of an editor.

Without question the article having the most popular appeal of all to young people is equally popular with editors of juveniles. It's the profile that deals with an outstanding boy or girl near their own ages. Perhaps a lad has distinguished himself athletically or a girl has an unusual hobby, or even someone is now working toward a goal he has set for himself and hopes to reach in the years ahead. The 12-15's all love this kind.

In the next chapter we study the profile in detail, showing how the same article, re-vamped, can sell three or more times. We shall also give an account of how to secure information for such articles. Here we are only introducing you to a sample profile.

The personality for this one was a colored girl in one of my high school classes, the profile appearing in a magazine for teen-agers. It is published here with the editor's permission.

And There Is Glory

When the members of the graduating class received their diplomas recently in a small Northeastern Pennsylvania high school, a frail little girl, tiniest in the group, heard herself named valedictorian. Although shy in nature and mildly spoken, Belle has won for herself an enviable place among her classmates.

But there was no envy, no evidence of surprise—nothing save commendation. Belle's learning ability is not all that they have recognized in her. She has contributed much to the school, has worked diligently for its best interests and theirs. Furthermore, she has throughout it all, suffered a trial her classmates couldn't appreciate. Belle is colored, the only one of her race among the entire student body.

Living in one of the large white houses for which the town is traditionally known, Belle occupies part of the "servants' quarters" in a physician's centrally located home. But hers is none of the glory of the big white house. She is as modest in dress as in disposition.

In her school activities Belle has found in her mother an interested partner. Almost daily the two have enjoyed walking together between school dismissal hour and the time her mother must be back to her domestic duties. Belle's face has usually been wreathed in smiles as she recounts to her eager listener the happenings of the day. Judging from her industriousness, there must always be plenty to relate, for Belle is the kind that puts much into school and therefore would get a lot out of school. ·

"Ever since I can remember," Belle says, "animals and insects have been an obsession with me. As a kid, worms, caterpillars, bugs, and tiny snakes came within an ace of being part of my diet." She confided to us later, however, that the sight of a crushed "pale green worm with orange horns" cured such gluttony. From a colored Easter chick to a pail of tadpoles—four stolen rabbits to a timid white mouse—Belle has lavished her affections on anything she could temporarily call a pet.

But none has ever won the place in her heart that Carla shares. Everyone who knows Belle knows Carla. For ten years the big, lumbering white dog has been her constant companion. "She's supposed to be a German Schnauzer," Belle told us, "but she is not supposed to have long hair. She was sort of a bargain." On the nature hikes that she so often takes, Carla shares half interest. The snakes Belle catches and takes home to tame, the caterpillars she finds and places in jars until they become moths are as common routine to Carla as the hike itself. "I dread to think about the future," confesses Belle, "because I know I shall lose her. Probably because of her age I do a lot of foolish things, such as stopping in the middle of the street until she gets safely across, or dodging an on-coming truck because I know the short-cut I've spotted will be easier on Carla's legs." Like Belle's friends, Carla senses that behind the friendly smile and large, rolling eyes, there's a certain firmness, a kind of stability that commands respect. A faithful companion, each would risk danger for the other.

But Belle's world is not one lived entirely to herself and dog. It is broader, in fact, than many of her schoolmates' experience. For her it has meant inward struggle toward social adjustment, but her popularity in high school has been evidence enough that she has succeeded. It has involved the conquering of a feeling of inferiority; and not only her scholastic standing but her long list of achievements proves her strength of determination.

Belle has been first clarinetist in her high school band, an organization that has won first place in Pennsylvania twenty-five times as well as honorable mention in national contests. In vocal music, as well, she has upheld the traditional reputation of her race. Like no other member of the girls' chorus, Belle has frequently held her audience electrified as the clear, plaintive tones of her solo would ring out: *"Were you there when they crucified my Lord?"* Belle has also been selected from that chorus for a girls' ensemble, appearing many times in public performances.

To mention that she was, during her last year, president of the high school Tri-Hi-Y club and editor-in-chief of the school paper puts her again in the category of the invaluables. No such recognition, though, came through chance. The title her classmates have fondly given her through the years—"the wheel"—is reason enough.

To give outward expression for what she has meant to her friends and the school was recently one of their proudest achievements. At a public high school assembly Belle was presented the D.A.R. Good Citizenship award, the first colored person to win such an honor in her state. The ceremony was unique in another respect; the presentation was made by a past Regent of the local chapter who had been a neighbor and friend of Belle's since the girl was six weeks old. Speaking in a low, musical voice with characteristic modesty and restraint, Belle acknowledged the award with a few simple words: "One of the first things I thought of, after I got over my surprise so I could think at all, was that the D.A.R. is an organization dedicated to the men who fought to found our country. And I feel that in receiving this pin I have seen real evidence of the kind of democracy those ancestors wanted for America."

One semester the high school students requested that a special dancing class be held during a portion of their regular noon hour. Upon investigation the instructor learned that the request was born purely out of a need felt by some three or four dozen students for self-improvement, and not, as she had suspected at first, for a free-for-all at the expense of her good nature. Not a few of the high school teachers were interested in learning just what students were willing to cut short their lunch period to fifteen minutes and hurry to the gym for a workout. They were not surprised, though, to see Belle, conspicuous among the others on the floor, her ears cued to the instructions as they came over the loud speaker. As the class was dismissed, Belle approached one of her instructors and said, "I'm glad we're going to have this class, for my dancing is pretty terrible, but I do feel sorry for the fellows that have to take their turn with me."

But if, through the years of training, there has been evidence of such humility, there has been a beauty of spirit, too. Belle seeks no pity, no favors. She asks only, in a spirit almost sacred, that tolerance continue. She would have you think of her not unlike the others.

Things to Do

Check yourself on the following, dealing with story writing.

(a) What new problem presents itself in writing for intermediates?

(b) Can a boys' story have a girl character in it?

(c) Can a girls' story have a boy character in it?

(d) Do we revise the plot formula for this age level?

(e) What is meant by "avoiding blackouts?"

(f) What is the test to good characterization?

(g) What is realism? Why should we include a bit of it in stories for this age and older?

(h) What are the three means of plunging into a story?

(i) How can we test an ending?

(j) What are the "taboo" subjects for juveniles?

Check yourself on these, dealing with article writing.

- (a) Why is article writing fertile territory for the beginning writer?
- (b) What dual purpose has the first paragraph of every article?
- (c) What are the five W's?
- (d) What danger may the writer face by not reading before he writes?
- (e) What two forms does the inspirational article take?
- (f) What is a profile?
- (g) What type of profile is most popular of all?

By referring to the story papers and magazines for intermediates, study the stories contained for these features:

- (a) How is the main character introduced? When?
- (b) How does the author plunge, through dialogue or what means?
- (c) What is the setting? story problem?
- (d) Who solved the problem?

Chapter 9

WRITING FOR
THE TEEN-AGERS

Stories

Much has been printed in both books and magazines on how to write and what to write for the senior group. Sixty per cent of it is wasted effort, for records prove that the older teens are interested, not in magazine stories appearing for their age level, but in novels and magazines intended for their parents.

In answer to questionnaires submitted to scores of these young folk, here were typical statements: "I just finished reading Hemingway." "Steinbeck is my favorite author." "Books on the best seller list make magazine stories seem pretty tame." "Mother and I always read the same stories."

It may be discouraging, then, at the outset, to consider story-writing for this group. True, we must not forget that there are all kinds of teen-agers with all sorts of backgrounds. Not all of them are too sophisticated to enjoy a teen-age book provided it is not juvenile in tone. Our possibilities lie, then, in writing for those whose reading background is more limited and whose environment, as well as inherent tendencies, has brought him through the teens still hungry for the finer things—if they really do reflect everyday life.

The 16-year-old and up is an exceptionally wise person. He can distinguish bluff from sincerity, fraud from honor. He observes, considers, decides. He is alert to changes, eager to conform, reluctant to be "different." He mingles with people, sizes them up, often without charity.

To cater to the interests of that age, then, the writer must be on his toes. He must adapt himself to the rapid changes that are taking place and turn out quality stuff in keeping with the trend.

Themes for the teens include very definitely the sports story with emphasis on football, baseball, and basketball. The career story, because of its significance to these part-time job holders, is always a favorite. Invention, science, history are of marked interest to many. And, of course, to keep up with the themes in popular magazines and books that these people have access to, we must include the elements of romance. Our best gauge as to the amount acceptable by editors is the careful study of magazines intended for the teen-agers. Mystery stories, yes, and adventure tales are always welcome.

To guarantee readable fiction for this group we must have a few vital features: (a) a good story

(b) early appearance of problem and suspense (c) a faster moving theme than that even for adults (d) strong characterization (e) accuracy of detail (f) an interesting style.

At least half of the elements just mentioned need a bit more discussion. A good story, for instance, is one that is sincere, timely, vivid; one that furnishes a vigorous and constructive slant on life. The bad story makes the good life seem dull and uninteresting.

In speaking of characterization—and this is repetition of what was said earlier—unless the characters in your story feel the conflict they are in, unless they see their problem and try to solve it, sense anxiety over the situation, become excited or bitter or desperate, your teen-age reader will sense "thinness" in your story.

Probably the most confusing term used in writing is style. To discuss it so that it can take on some "earthy" meaning, let us recall what was said about titles. At that time we compared a good title with an attractive store window display, obviously the striking, colorful one serving best for sales promotion. Style should be regarded in much the same way, for it, too, is the "window dressing" which will attract readers to "try it" or "pass it up."

Now that does not imply that one should adopt a fancy, superficial means of expression in order to invite and hold attention, for the result will very definitely be just the opposite; you will not hold! A writer can correct his weaknesses; he can improve his sentence structure; he can check his spelling,

punctuation, and diction with a dictionary and reliable guide; he can learn proper techniques of writing;
but his style represents his own individuality! It
should permeate his story just as his personality is
recognized among his friends. It should be sort of
a warmth, a friendliness, that kindles a pleasant
atmosphere.

When a juvenile finds a story "dull"; when he
says, "It's preachy"; when he discovers that "it doesn't
sound real"; or when "it drags," he is telling the
world what is wrong with the author's style!

The key to good writing is simplicity and clarity. The technical textbook calls for study, concen-
tration; the work of fiction, on the contrary, should
offer entertainment without a struggle as to the
meaning. Again the warning: "Don't write down to
be clear!" Again the plea: "Read! Study the present
day writing that is good and your own efforts will
unconsciously reflect an element that will ring true."

The beginner is and probably should be uncon-
scious of style when he first sets out to get a story
on paper. But once the first draft is finished and he
has told his story, created his characters, and attempted
to put feeling into his writing, he is ready to think
about polishing. He should look at his work criti-
cally, asking himself: "Have I been clear?" "Have I
been 'wordy'?" "Does that dialogue sound natural?"
"Does this scene drag?" "Is this the right word?"
"Is that description too long?" "Have I said what
I intended to say?" Simultaneously, he is developing
style by working for simplicity and clarity.

AIDS TO EXPRESSIVENESS

As one means of assuring clarity, we recall the need for using punch-giving verbs. In fact, our choice of them should head the list of aids toward effective writing. Note the sense impressions we create when we choose our verbs with care. *The churned-up water frothed alongside the boat.* Or this one: *A droning bee blundered into a swarm of tiny, jigging gnats.*

The writer also can make very effective use of figurative language. Since it is a very easy matter to overdo, making a muddy impression of a transparent one, the beginning writer should exercise discretion in its use.

We cannot go through the long list of figures of speech in common use thoroughly here. We do believe, however, that to review a few of the most common ones might prove valuable. After all, the teen-agers in high school today are familiar with their use so it would behoove the writer of juveniles to speak the language they know.

1. Simile   (comparison of two unlike things using *like* or *as*)

    a. Her mind was like a weathervane.
    b. The cold was as sharp as a razor.

2. Metaphor   (comparison without the use of
   like or *as*)

   a. Her eyes were pools of fire.
   b. Contentment is a pearl of great
      price.

3. Personification   (attributing life to inani-
   mate things)

   a. The moon veiled her face with
      a cloud.
   b. April smiled through her tears.

4. Antithesis   (balanced contrast)

   a. To err is human; to forgive,
      divine.
   b. We are not machines, but men.

5. Metonymy   (The use of the name of one
   thing for the name of another
   it clearly suggests)

   a. He prefers a golf club (pleasure)
      to a hoe. (work)
   b. The pen (writing) is mightier
      than the sword (war).

6. Hyperbole   (Exaggeration for the sake of
   emphasis)

    a. His hands dangled a mile out of his sleeves.

    b. A million wrinkles carved his skin.

7. Interrogation (A question to which one expects no answer)

    a. Who is not proud to be an American?

    b. How could he do such a thing?

8. Onomatopoeia (Use of a word that imitates action or sound)

    a. "Tick-tock, tick-tock" went the old clock on the mantlepiece.

    b. The buzzing bees interrupted her dream.

Figures of speech arouse the reader's imagination and memory; they appeal to his senses; they create in him a close association of himself with the details and characters in the story. In short, they make the reader live the story. When you have done that for anyone, adult or juvenile, you have learned to write!

Articles

What has been implied at least twice in earlier chapters we repeat here most emphatically: For every piece of fiction that often takes a week or two to conceive, write, and polish, the beginning writer can match in four hours with article writing. (But if you're more interested in story-writing, stick to it!

Besides, he has a more readily available pattern to follow (depending on the type of article he is interested in), does not have to invent his subject, and can establish himself as a regular writer far more quickly than can the writer of stories.

The fact that *Reader's Digest* furnishes students' copies which have been adopted as part of the English curriculum in hundreds of American schools is proof enough that the teen-agers' field is the "big acre" for the writer of articles.

THE BEGINNING

We have already learned that a good introductory paragraph serves a dual purpose: (1) to catch the reader's interest and (2) to lead to the core of the article. So very much depends on those opening lines that we feel it imperative to give this phase of article writing more study before proceeding. So just to make sure that you understand what constitutes a good beginning and to help you see the various devices that can guarantee eye-catching interest of the reader, we print here a few for your study and analysis.

In this first one you will notice that the question method has been used, one of the ways of "hooking" the reader. Sometimes it is difficult to grip our reader with the very first sentence, but we must not fail to do so somewhere in the first paragraph. It is, of course, infinitely better if we can give the master stroke at the outset.

> Did you know that at one time men paid $50 a piece for their linen shirts? Did you know that they were intended only for the wealthy? And did you know that back in the tenth century their shirts were the exact pattern from which your T shirts are cut?

No teen-ager is going to slip by this one with its brevity and unusual fact.

> William Austin, a sixteen-year-old school boy of Blankville, Massachusetts, has a most unusual hobby. He keeps a hive of 75,000 bees in his bedroom.

With a "starter" like this, the writer has already aroused the curiosity of his reader.

> Be sure to take your kit of tools with

you when you apply for that first part-time
job.

Here, too, the reader finds himself saying, "What
are they?"

> In the mountain range that separates
> Los Angeles from the fertile valley of the
> sun to the North, strange things are taking
> place.

This is the introduction I used in an article on
sledge dogs one time, *Heroes of the Wild.* See how
quickly the reader is brought to the scene of action.

> "Mush!" cries the driver, and to every-
> one familiar with the Far North that signal
> means but one thing. The dog teams are
> ready, the sleds have been packed with pro-
> visions, and the long journey across the
> barren tract is about to begin. It may be
> that they will encounter deep drifts or tem-
> perature that falls to seventy degrees below
> zero. But these huskies of the Arctic have
> no fear. Their courage and endurance are a
> natural part of them in this country where
> it is so hard to survive.

The thought-provoking question opened this article
of mine, "What Tree So Fair?" mentioned in an
earlier chapter.

Have you ever asked yourself why a tree, glistening with its golden stars and lights on imitation frost-trimmed boughs, should be a symbol of the holiest celebration of the Christians?

If you choose to employ the fictional beginning, make sure that you plunge immediately into the story. This was one I chose for a teen-age-level article.

The Otter Woman turned and with stern face eyed the new Indian girl. Sacajawea, busy husking the golden corn, paid no attention. The brisk October air snapped at her slender brown legs as the wind swept through the tall rows. But Sacajawea paid little attention to that either.

Sadly she looked toward the distant horizon. The purple mountains with their jagged rocks and ledges seemed so far away this afternoon. A feeling of emptiness seized her. It was as though the other eight slaves were not there at all. "It might be," she mused, looking wistfully out over the wide expanse between herself and the distant hills, "that some day—over there—I shall be taken back." She clutched her throat tightly for a moment, that no sob should escape to the ears of those near by.

THE 7 DO'S IN ARTICLE WRITING

1. Prepare more notes than you use. (What you don't use will give you moral support anyhow.)
2. Pack the article with interest.
3. Entertain as well as inform.
4. Filter the style of your article with facts and drama and a touch of dialogue.
5. Maintain a conversational tone.
6. Work for exactness and clarity.
7. Weed out unnecessary details.

THE ENDING

We have already pointed out that the ending is the hardest feature of an article to teach. In the previous chapter we listed test questions which might serve as a guide to measure the quality of that ending.

Here, let us add, that the article popular with the teen-ager is delivered with a punch. Whether it be dramatic, of question and answer nature, a generalization, or a promise, it must close in tone and content with that which has gone before.

Here is the final paragraph of the article on sledge dogs.

Today the urge to race is on them

again. The driver has picked up the reins, and with a wave and a "cheerio" to those who watch the departure, has stepped up on the rear of the sled. "Mush!" he shouts, and the dog team, led by faithful Spunky, is off to another adventure in the frozen North.

And here is the final paragraph of the article earlier referred to, "What Tree So Fair?"

Many churches in America have come to use it as an integral part of their Sunday School festivities. As a symbol of peace the older members of the congregation regard it. For many of the youngsters at the cross-roads, the "church tree" is the only real Christmas they have. Truly the world has come to say with the poet—

What tree so fair,
So bright, so free—
A symbol of peace
To humanity!

In both cases we obviously have a tie-in, a blending of the theme as given in the opening lines. And that is the all-important feature of good endings!

In this chapter it is our aim to present (1) another type of fact article that teen-agers have expressed a keen interest in, the one dealing with history of something and (2) also furnish a more thorough study of what profile writing involves and offers. The first example was referred to in Chapter 5 when I explained how it happened to be written.

THE HISTORY FACT ARTICLE

What Time Is Your English?

Had you ever thought how hard it might be to carry on a conversation if you were to step back a century for just one day? You couldn't say "hello" to your friends, since *hello* did not appear in our language until 1850. You'd own no *wrist-watch, poodle,* nor *typewriter;* neither could you buy a *coke* at a *restaurant.* You couldn't send a *telegram* nor see a *smokestack.* You wouldn't be wearing *pajamas,* eating *spaghetti* or *goulash,* nor looking at *snapshots. Poinsettias* wouldn't yet have bloomed (the word arrived in 1867) nor would you walk on *linoleum.* You could have a terribly sore throat, but it wouldn't have been *tonsilitis.* Yes, these and countless other words are much newer than one might realize.

Most of you have probably read *Uncle Tom's Cabin* or have seen the play. If so, you will remember Topsy, the little colored girl who was always finding herself in some kind of trouble. Somebody asked her one day where she was born. "Ah wasn't nevah bohned," she said. "Ah just growed."

Very much like Topsy is the language we speak

today. It never really was born anywhere. It has just grown. It has borrowed more words than almost any other language, yet through those words we have come to understand much of the life of the people who first spoke them.

Probably our greatest number came from Anglo-Saxon, the language spoken by a race of fair, blue-eyed people from the mainland of Europe who settled on the island of Britain some 1500 years ago. They lived on farms and in towns, banding together in clans for protection. Gradually they gained control of almost all of Britain.

Since those Anglo-Saxons for the most part lived very simple lives, most of their words stood for common, everyday things. They wrote their records on slabs of beech wood, bound together and called boc, their word for beech. From this word came our word *book*.

Their word for *butter* was "cow cheese." Their idea of bread is perhaps a little harder to under-stand. Unlike the separate food we think of, they used the word to indicate food left from a meal; in other words, bread meant "fragment." *Thumb* comes from a word meaning "swollen finger."

Even the common field daisy had its name given to it by those early settlers. To them the yellow center looked like the sun, and since the sun is really the eye of the day, they called the flower by a name meaning "day's eye."

In the language of those same Saxons we have had preserved for us a copy of the Lord's Prayer, written about 700 A.D. In it you can detect many words that look almost like our own. Then again, it is interesting to see how through the years a perfectly good word like "the" would be "which" or "who" to us today.

Thu ure Fader, the eart on heafonum
Si thin noman gehalgod.
Cume thin rice.
Si thin Willa on earthan twa on heofonum
Syle us todag orne daogwanlican hlef,
And forgif us ure gylter
Swa we forgifath them the with us agylthat;
And ne laed thu na us on kostunge
Ac abys from yfele. Si bit swa.

Thou our Father, who art in heaven,
Be Thy name hallowed.
Come Thy Kingdom.
So Thy will on earth 'twas in Heaven
Give us today our daily bread
And forgive us our guilt
As we forgiveth those who against us perform guilt;
And lead Thou not us into temptation
But deliver us from evil. So be it.

Our language is especially rich because of the contributions from other tongues as well. Not only the nations with thousands of years of civilization behind them, but even the semi-civilized and the uncivilized have added to our store of words. In the most ordinary of sentences we may happen to use words from a surprising combination of sources.

Notice the variety of languages from which we borrow in sentences such as these:

	Dutch	A-Saxon		Latin	A-Saxon
The	etching	showed	the	soldier	seated

	A-Saxon	A-Saxon			Dutch
on the stone	wall	with	his	knapsack
beside him.

N.A. Indian			French	Latin	Italian
Hominy	is	my	favorite	cereal,	artichokes

	French		A-Saxon	A-Saxon
the vegetables	I	like	best.

A fascinating phase of our language lies in the change that has come about in the meaning of many ordinary words. Because John Duns Scotus held different religious beliefs from those of his college chums, his name has become a term of ridicule and reproach to us. He was in the minority at school, and the majority made fun of him and his followers, who were called Dunsmen. A Duns became a *dunce.* In reality Duns was an illustrious teacher, acknowledged to have been a keen and subtle thinker.

To our ears the word *pantaloons* is homely, a bit humorous in connotation, too. But it originated in Venice when fashion introduced a new cut of long hose. The patron saint of Venice was St. Pantaloone; the new Venetian garment was called *pantaloons.*

We accept the fact that language undergoes changes by invention, industry, and war. In our own century that change has been the most rapid of all periods. This should not be surprising when one senses that the vocabulary has swelled through such mediums as radio, television, movies, aviation, the automobile, medicine, space programs. Some words, especially the technical ones, are slower to be adopted than others. (Perhaps there's some advantage in this. No automobile, no blow-out; no dictator, no underdog; no union, no striker.)

It is clear, then, that the English vocabulary grows each year, just as an oak tree adds a ring. Great-grandma said *fetch, methinks,* and *trode.* But then Grandma wore hoop skirts and chemisettes. Our English must be the English of our time.

(Reprinted with permission of the publishers)

THE PROFILE

And now for one of the most popular types of articles for this age level, the profile.

Biographical material of this sort is not difficult to find. In Chapter 5 I showed how the study of one weekly newspaper furnished me with four subjects (and incidentally, six articles and stories, plus cash). Referring to that chapter, you will note the profile we are using as a "case" article is the one mentioned in that discussion.

Needless to say, then, that newspapers are the

easiest and cheapest sources for such article subjects. But, you ask, suppose I do read in a newspaper an account of some young person's outstanding
achievement; perhaps the lad lives miles away. Should
I expect to get all the details by correspondence?
Certainly. As I pointed out previously, the writer's
safest bet, after getting permission to use him as
a subject for an article, is to submit a carefully
constructed questionnaire that will furnish you with
what you want to know. After all, from his view-
point, certain features might seem unimportant or
he might be too modest to make admissions.

Naturally, the questionnaire will depend upon
what you already learned from the newspaper article
or from the facts as told you.

Let's study the development of this profile, see
what we worked from and where we ended with
it. First, the little newspaper clipping contained
these facts: (1) Arden T., a high school junior was
playing his second season of varsity baseball; (2)
a splendid athlete, though handicapped by an arm
amputation; (3) regular left fielder position demon-
strated clever ingenuity in catching the ball; (4) hitting average above the .300 mark (5) even more
outstanding, the boy's spirit which has made him a
foremost personality in his high school. With that
information clipped from the paper, I had only the
nucleus for a profile.

Here is the questionnaire I submitted to the
young high school lad and with it (in parentheses)
the answers his mother furnished.

Birth   date:
        (Oct. 26, 19——)

Height:
        (5 feet 10 inches)

Weight:
        (136   pounds)

At what age did accident happen?
        ($3\frac{1}{2}$ years)

How?
        (Fell 12 ft. in barn)

How long was he in the hospital?
        (6 weeks; infection set in, making it im-
        possible to save arm)

Can you recall some things that were hardest for him
when he was small to make the adjustment?
        (To tie his shoe strings or his tie have
        always bothered him. Other things he
        has overcome as he became old enough
        to do them.)

Nickname?
        (Joe, and prefers it to his name)

Can you identify traits of his disposition with any of these? Check those that apply to him.

        Timid
        Quiet
  x Makes friends easily
  x Ambitious
        Witty
        Even-tempered
  x Willful
        Revengeful
        A tease
        Moody
  x Any time for girls?
  x Systematic about duties?
  x Neat about his work?
  x Carefree

Has he learned to operate a tractor?
      (Yes)

Drive a car?
      (Yes)

Ride horseback?
      (Yes)

Hunt?
      (Yes)

Fish?
      (Yes)

Does he have any pets?
>   (No)

If so, what?

Favorite subject in high school?
>   (History)

Any subject or subjects that are difficult for him?
>   (No)

Does he like music?
>   (Yes)

Sing?
>   (No)

Play a musical instrument?
>   (Yes, trumpet)

Does he like to read?
>   (Yes)

Attend church?
>   (Yes)

Member of a church?
>   (Yes)

Has he ever earned money for himself?
>   (Yes)

If so, how?

> (4 H projects; Ag projects; is janitor of
> the community Grange Hall)

Does he have any hobby outside sports?
> (No)

Any achievement other than those mentioned above?
> (Can swim)

Has he ever engaged in any extra-curricular activities
besides sports?
> (No)

Who is his "hero" in the sports world?
> (2 or 3 were named)

Are there any little incidents through his early childhood, or even later, that stand out in your mind,
perhaps because they were cute, touching, amusing,
etc.? If so, could you cite them?
> (2 or 3 were furnished)

What comments have neighbors ever made about him?
> (They are always amazed at his ability
> to do farm work with the rest. He works
> right along with the men at all kinds
> of jobs, running the milking machines,
> haying, threshing, etc.)

With the accumulation of these facts and the
newspaper information, I developed this first article.

You will notice that the fictional method is used throughout and also that not every detail furnished by the boy's mother was included in the article.

The writer should never feel that he must use all the material available; the practice often results in an overcrowding of detail that is not good. Furthermore, what is left out of one article may be included in a second with a little different slant and treatment. Here is how my first article appeared. (Reprinted here with permission of the publishers)

Heir to Honor

He stood with unusual calm—this sixteen-year-old boy at the batter's box—awaiting the first pitch. Over the spectators that afternoon a strange sense of awe suddenly settled. Even the eyes of the umpire betrayed an interest akin to curiosity.

"You mean he's up to bat?" whispered a girl on the front row of the bleachers. "That boy?"

The coach smiled blandly as his glance met those of his reserves. It was obvious that their thoughts were alike. Here was Joe, "ready to show 'em."

The appearance of sparky little Joe T— in a baseball uniform is a familiar sight to the people of his home town. But today, visiting a rival team's "camp ground," the crowd wasn't quite ready for it. The fact that Joe has but one arm seemed a handicap.

Firmly he grasped the bat in his left hand and eyed the pitcher. Then the wind-up came, and the throw. Ball one. Joe dug his foot a little deeper in the ground. "Let's have it, boy!" shouted the next fellow in line. And in less than seconds Joe had come through. A long drive out over center field, out—out—no, the fielder doesn't get it—and the plucky little runner was rounding second. "Go it!" shouted his team-mates. Then Joe slowed cautiously to third.

With mouths wide open, the friends of the opposing team looked on bewildered. There was no denying it; the cheers that went up from the crowd at that moment came from both sides of the bleachers. But his own team accepted the play calmly, confidently. They knew what he could do, for the record Joe has made for himself is excellent. His strong left arm has kept his hitting average above the .300 mark. And as their coach had so aptly expressed it on many occasions, "Joe's will-to-win in any contest is the unseen force behind the entire high school team."

Yes, an outsider watching Joe play for the first time soon realizes how expertly he has overcome his handicap. Besides, as regular outfielder for his team, he has a fielding average far above that of many of his teammates. His method of catching the ball in his left hand, rolling it into the crook of his arm, pulling his glove off under the stub of his right arm, and throwing the ball—all in the time it takes to wink— leaves the opposing team and their fans speechless.

His buddies, sensing the surprise of the crowd as they view the almost incredulous spectacle, waste little time in adding further praise. "If you think this is good, you should see him play basketball," they announce. "He's the reason we win there, too."

And it's true. The one-armed center throughout the game seems to supply the spark that ignites the team's action. His speedy plays and smooth ball handling make it possible very frequently to jab the best defensive set-up on the floor. The "oh's" and "ah's" from spectators when Joe, with perfect control and lightning speed, dribbles that ball down the floor and tosses it to the forward for a field goal, reveal sharply the appreciation of his skill. But quite in contrast is the hush that falls on the crowd as Joe takes his place on the foul line. With firm, even perception and a particular poising of the ball between his left hand and the stub of his other arm, he invariably comes through for a foul shot. "The best morale builder I could ask for," says the coach. And nobody puts up an argument.

But amazed as the crowds are at Joe's ball playing, even more outstanding to them is his spirit. The fact is, his entire boyhood has been woven around a constant and courageous battle, especially when the outdoor life that he loves has been sought after with the odds mounted sky-high against him.

Joe, you see, was victim of an accident when he was three and a half. Playing in the barn with two of his older brothers, he lost his footing and fell twelve feet to the floor below, breaking his right arm at the elbow. When an infection set in a few days later, surgeons despaired of saving him unless immediate amputation was performed.

His mother recalls very vividly his return from the long stay in the hospital. Home at last and realizing things were different for him from now on, he pointed to his shoulder one day and asked timidly of her, "When are they gonna put it back on?" Strangely enough, though, when the full realization of his plight dawned on him and he learned they "were never gonna put it back on," Joe faced the facts bravely.

During the long period of making adjustments, the youngster built for himself the dream of living a normal, happy, useful life like others. "I'll make it," he told himself countless times. And today the bare facts of the case prove him right.

Joe drives a car as capably as anyone. That tractor which his father bought a few years ago hasn't proved itself a hurdle for him, either. His ability to do general farm work has amazed everyone, for he takes his place along with the others, whether it's threshing, haying, or operating the milking machine. Furthermore, he has earned a neat little sum for himself through 4 H projects, Ag projects, and as janitor at the village Grange hall.

Nor has Joe allowed himself to be denied the sports his friends enjoy. He rides a horse well, loves to fish, and has become an excellent swimmer. Probably the hardest feat he has accomplished is that of manipulating his 30-40 rifle; but, like most boys, he's a "lover of the chase" and has bagged several deer and considerable small game since he learned to handle a gun.

When Joe approached the band director of his high school a few years ago, telling him he'd like to learn a musical instrument, he was greeted with an expression not far from hopelessness. Hesitantly the director asked him if he had any preference. "Well," replied Joe with the customary good-natured grin, "if I can handle a gun, I ought to be able to handle a trumpet, don't you think?" The director didn't think. "Mounds of difficulty," he was saying to himself, "almost as unsurpassable as those in *Pilgrim's Progress.*" But aloud he said as jovially as he could, "We can try it." It took a little ingenuity on Joe's part to determine just how to hold the instrument securely, but once settled on the method, he eagerly applied himself to the new task. It may be because Joe has an abundance of ambition, or perhaps it's the systematic way he goes about a job, but somehow, everything he tackles is done with a will that knows no limit. His trumpet playing is no exception. When others marvel at his many accomplishments, he merely says, "Well, why not? One arm is hardly an inconvenience any more."

A carefree, graceful lad, Joe makes friends easily both in and out of school. Fond of history, music, and books in general, he is succeeding in just what he set out to do long ago: live a full, well-rounded life—one he can enjoy and be proud of. His friends will tell you he's doing a better job of it than many of them. To ask Joe the secret, you'll get only one answer: "If you think you're beaten, you are." But putting the question squarely before him— "What holds number one interest for you?"

—it's fun to watch his eyes light up and the broad smile creep over his face as he says, "Silly question. Baseball, of course."

But this was only the beginning—which brings us to a phase of writing not yet touched upon in these chapters—squeezing the sponge dry. Frequently there is enough material in our notes on a subject to furnish us with the second editor's check. Just as frequently, by re-vamping the style of our article toward the market we aim to hit, we can use those same facts the second and third time.

Now using the same material (from the news clipping and the questionnaire), and arranging those facts in a little different order, I turned it from a fictional profile to a feature article. Here it is in part as it appeared in a Sunday supplement.

What may well be considered the most courageous sports review in our section of the state spotlights a sixteen-year-old Blankville High School lad, Arden T. Whether it's in basketball or baseball, when sparky little "Joe" (as he prefers to be called) appears on the scene, a strange sense of awe suddenly settles on the spectators. The fact that he has but one arm seems to them a handicap.

But Joe this past season of basketball has proved they're wrong, for the scorebook shows he piled up a total of 157 points, a figure exceeding that of many of his teammates and members of rival teams. Through-out the game the wiry little one-armed center seems to supply the spark that ignites the team's action. His speedy plays and smooth ball-handling make it possible very frequently to jab the best defensive set-up on the floor.

Yes, the "ah's" and "oh's" from specta-tors when Joe, with perfect control and light-ning speed, dribbles that ball down the floor and tosses it to the forward for a field goal, reveal sharply an appreciation of his skill. But quite in contrast is the hush that falls on the crowd as Joe takes his place on the foul line. With firm, even perception and a particular poising of the ball between his left hand and the stub of his other arm, he invariably comes through for a foul shot.

But we still have within our rights further possibilities of using such material. Boiling down the facts to a 700 word précis and re-slanting the story, we squeezed the sponge still further—this time to appear in *Boy Who Hit the Mark* column of a teen-age paper. This is the way it appeared in part.

"If you think you're beaten, you are," was the slogan aptly adopted by a little six-year-old several years ago. Today the envia-ble record which sixteen-year-old Arden T—, a northeastern Pennsylvania high school lad, holds among his associates is proof enough that that spirit still prevails.

The fact that "Joe," as he prefers to be called, lost an arm in a childhood accident, did not loom as a handicap to the boy who loved sports better than food. Fellows on the baseball team can't appreciate the struggle it has meant for him, but they can appreciate his better than .300 hitting average. They also know something of the lightning speed Joe displays as regular outfielder, a feat that frequently leaves spectators gasping.

In basketball, too, the wiry little chap excels.

Things to Do

1. Study as many short stories currently published as possible, taking notes on plot, action, and characters as you do so. Occasionally outline the author's plot.

2. Select from a current newspaper some item that might lend itself to a juvenile article. The editorial page often furnishes excellent ideas for such work. Try the opening paragraph in several different ways: the question method, fiction method, etc.

3. From your newspaper clipping file, select a subject that you think would have appeal to the senior group—perhaps of historical interest—and

begin reading up on the subject. Take plenty of notes as you do your research. When you have your material collected and organized, develop in your own style a 1000-word article. Work especially hard for (a) an eye-catching beginning, (b) selection of interesting details, (c) a little drama or dialogue, (d) blended ending.

4. By this time you undoubtedly have in your notebook at least one subject for a profile. It can be either an adult whose life or work is inspiring to youth, or another teen-ager whose accomplishments are worthy of your writing effort. Following the questionnaire method for securing material (or personal interview if possible) secure all the information you can on your subject. That done, develop in fictional style a 1000-word profile. After your first draft is completed, turn again to several teen-age published articles and read them carefully. Then re-read your own article and revise where necessary.

Chapter 10

HOW TO SELL
WHAT YOU WRITE

To write and then "hope to sell what we write" is, of course, putting the cart before the horse. The time to plan a sale for our work is the day we sit down to plan our story or article. First, then, looms the question: How salable is the idea?

Granted, we are not infallible; we can easily misjudge a situation, believing our ideas perfect and having the bewildering "thumbs down" experience follow. In my own experience I have sold what might be termed "practice exercises" when I least expected to; but on the other hand, I wrote a 3000-word article one time that I still believe the best thing that came out of my typewriter that year, only to submit it to 14 editors before I learned that it was not the style of the piece, but the underlying idea that was creating a question. For the most part, though, it is our responsibility as salesmen to analyze the product, study its features, and make our decisions early—not build false hopes that are bound to crash all for the lack of forethought on our part.

After we have settled the issue, then, of the suitability of idea, we must consider its appeal. Can it be made interesting? What age readers will be attracted to it? Is there a buying public? Have we read enough in that age level field to warrant faith in our own work? If, by a conscientious study of our efforts, we can answer in the affirmative, the green light is ours.

Your success at writing depends upon constant work and tireless salesmanship. As a writer you are in the mail-order business. "If you write ten stories and have to send each of them to ten editors before they sell, you should, by the law of averages, sell at least three," was the opinion of a writing teacher several years ago. Your average today should be a lot better. Editors' needs are publicized; writers' magazines offer up-to-date market tips; the writer who wants to sell has learned he must study markets as well as write for them.

Naturally, the better established you become, the higher will be your percentage of sales. It all boils down to a matter of quantity production and aggressive marketing, for success in this business of writing, as in everything else, is cumulative.

The question of an agent always arises when the subject of manuscript sales comes up. For the beginning writer of juvenile material it is unnecessary provided the writer is willing to study his markets. A surprising number of top-notch authors today have never employed one, yet often the new-comer in the field seems to think himself incapable of writing and selling. Learn to be independent. Have confidence in your ability, in your wares. Don't lean on a crutch even for moral support. It is difficult to interest an agent in short, juvenile material anyhow. The reputable agent is much more likely to be on the lookout for good book-length stuff.

SLANTING YOUR MATERIAL

Everyone wants to sell what he writes, but unfortunately he often adopts the reverse procedure —that of writing a story and then sending it out to an editor hit or miss. To slant a story means to write it with a definite magazine in mind. For amateurs this would be too rigid, too expensive an ordeal. But he can slant to a particular field such as intermediate girls, juniors, etc.

The first step is, of course, what was suggested in Chapter 3, that of securing sample copies of juvenile magazines and story papers and study what the editors are buying. The fairest and most accurate way of learning the proper slant is to study two or three issues of the same magazine.

Some teachers even advocate that the very best way to understand an author's slant is to type it word for word directly from the juvenile paper. Somehow, they believe one gets the feel of the writing and learns the process more forcibly this way. I've never done it myself, but I have traced outlines from stories for the same purpose.

By a conscientious study of a magazine, you will find slant a relatively easy matter if you keep in mind what those authors heeded: namely, correct vocabulary level, children's interests, avoiding the "writing down" temptation.

You need a ready market list. Study it carefully rather than mail out stories promiscuously.

HOW TO PREPARE THE MANUSCRIPT

If every writer could take a glance at the busy editor's desk and see the true picture of what really takes place in his office as piles of articles, stories, and poetry are collecting, he would quickly conclude that the certain commandments of manuscript preparation should be compulsory.

The instructions that follow are not a matter of courtesy and neatness; they are the indispensable means of furthering your chances for an acceptance from the editor. Believe them; heed them. Remember your manuscript is your salesman. Impress your editor!

1. Type your name and address, single spaced, in the upper left corner on the first page.

2. Record the length in the upper right corner of the first page. For example, 800 words. (The mark of an amateur is to count as closely as 811 words; always keep the figure in round numbers.) Underneath that number write *Usual rates*.

3. Be sure that the manuscript is typed (not hand written) neatly. If you can't type, hire a competent typist for 50¢ a 1000 words.

4. Use good quality paper 8½ x 11 inches; thin stock may cost slightly less but it will not withstand travel. By the time a fuzzy-edged manuscript has had eight rejections, what chance has the last editor to read it without being biased?

5. Keep the type face clean; avoid dirt-filled letters. Use a black ribbon.

6. Leave 1½ inch margins at both sides and type the title in capital letters at least one-third of the way down from the top. If you don't wish to use your real name, under the title write By .... (whatever you select for a substitute).

7. Be sure you are correct in spelling, punctuation, and capitalization. (Editors tell us that no phase of the mechanics of writing so irks them to the point of rejecting manuscripts as faulty punctuation and capitalization.)

8. All manuscripts MUST be double spaced on one side only of the paper.

9. Always make carbon copies of manuscripts.

10. Number the pages (after the first) in the upper right corner. In other words start by writing the figure 2 on page 2. Do not place periods after the numerals.

11. Manuscripts of story or article length (not book) should be sent first class. If not too bulky, they can be folded into thirds and mailed in long envelopes. If, however, there is a photograph accompanying the article, or if the manuscript is bulky, it should be mailed flat in a 9x12 or 6x9 envelope. Be sure to enclose a stamped envelope of sufficient size to provide for its return in case the editor rejects it.

12. Carry out standard paragraph indentions throughout the manuscript. The typists' rule of five or six spaces is adequate.

13. Avoid stapling sheets together. The pages should be loose but arranged in order when placed in envelope.

14. Send your manuscripts out "dressed up" but not fancy. Besides the neat kraft envelope, use a business-looking address label carefully typed to the editor. All such details go a long way in making

a favorable impression on the man who says *Yes* or *No*.

15. If you want words to appear in italics, underscore them.

16. Keep your manuscripts neat and clean. If they are returned to you soiled and rumpled, re-type the pages that need it.

WHAT SHOULD THE WRITER'S LIBRARY CONTAIN?

I am not a book agent and represent no company that sells merchandise for writers. I have no affiliations with magazines other than as a contributor to them. But from an experience that has extended over several years, I consider certain books for writers an essential part of their equipment. I believe a handy shelf near that working desk of theirs should contain what I call the Big Nine. I am convinced they are a source from which the writer of juveniles can draw for inspiration and information when the need arises.

Often the beginning writer cannot afford to buy all these at the start, but he probably can do so at various intervals and should if he is serious about this job of writing. They are as vital to him as his typewriter.

1. A Good Dictionary I have used several but lean most heavily toward Webster's Student Dictionary for upper school levels.

2. **The Holy Bible** No more beautiful literature in any classic can be found than that in the "best seller" of all time. Its graceful phrasing, its rhythm, its figures of speech, its beautiful simplicity —yes, even for situations—it has served as inspiration for many writers.

3. **Roget's Thesaurus of English Words and Phrases** This is the standard book of words, a time-saver and handy reference for both the writer of fiction and non-fiction. Available at book stores.

4. **A Handbook on Punctuation and Capitalization** Even a small paperback reference similar to that used by stenographers is better than nothing.

5. **A Good Market Guide** No one can possibly be successful at writing and selling if he is unacquainted with the current needs and demands of the many juvenile editors. Besides the market lists appearing frequently in various writers' magazines, there are several very fine books available, one of which should be on every writer's desk. Probably those best known are *Writer's Market,* The *Writer's Handbook,* and *Literary Market Place.*

6. **The Horn Book Magazine** An invaluable aid for the writer of juveniles. Through its pages, he can follow the trend of modern juvenile stories; he can acquaint himself with successful writers and the type of work each is producing; it can serve as a challenge to good taste in our writing.

7. Huckleberry Finn Every writer for children should set for himself the goal of matching the qualities in the world's best loved children's book. It is by far the finest example of its kind (first person) for any writer.

8. Free Bulletin and Price List of Pamphlets Issued by the United States Government For a nominal sum (often 5¢) the writer of articles can find an inexhaustive source of material from which to draw. By writing to Supt. of Documents, Washington, D.C., the writer can secure the free bulletin.

9. At least one good writer's magazine Books offer standard practices of writing and the long-range view so necessary for the student to grasp if he expects to fit into the picture acceptably. Magazines furnish one with the up-to-date tricks of the trade, pass on the results of recent explorations into the publishers' offices, and hand on to us the practical discoveries authors have made in their various fields.

WHAT ABOUT PICTURES?

You have undoubtedly heard the ancient Chinese proverb, "A picture is worth a thousand words." From many editors there is a hearty "Amen" response to that statement. If you want proof, start gleaning the magazines and story papers for all ages.

Now there are two general types of illustrations: art work and photographs. Art work includes pen drawings, sketches, designs, blue prints, painting, etc.

If one does not have suitable camera equipment to provide his own photos, he can often make arrangements with a photographer or advanced amateur to take pictures for him. Though on the surface it may appear to eat into the profits of the beginning writer, he may soon discover that he cannot afford to sell articles without them. True, there are many editors who handle their own illustration work. Therefore one must be careful to study the market to avoid submitting an article with or without a photo, as the case of that particular publisher demands.

If one desires to do so, he can purchase through a reliable agency any number of beautiful gloss prints for $1.00 and $1.50 each. There are many syndicates that offer this service.

It is very possible that the writer can take his own pictures, but in any case they must be clear, simple, and tell a story. Most editors prefer 5x7 or 8x10 gloss prints, not negatives. A photo accompanying an article may often mean the difference between acceptance and rejection of the writer's work. The how-to-do almost always demands an illustration in the form of a glossy print showing the completed project. Occasionally the various steps of the procedure need to be shown, as well. Photos are likewise important in selling hobby articles, profiles, features. Human interest pictures are the best, especially those which show people in characteristic pose. Never have your subject looking at the camera.

DO'S FOR WRITERS

1. Be systematic about your work. And system includes gathering facts, filing and indexing reference material, and in following a writing schedule. It even includes a sales book or card file in which you list the title of story or article that has been mailed out, date of submission, what magazine, and what happened to it. Some writers divide their card files into three sections: Out, Sold, and Rejected.

2. Read your stories and articles aloud; then try them out on a juvenile. Many a writer has rewritten her stuff after she found that the audience reception was poor.

3. Send out seasonal material (Christmas, Easter, etc.) five months in advance.

4. Keep manuscripts in the mail all the time! (Some article writers have as many as 500 in circulation.)

5. If, after studying juvenile publications, you find one or two that publish just the kind of material you are interested in writing, it will pay you to subscribe for a year to those publications. (They cost only a few cents each.)

6. Believe in your story if you know it is helpfully and interestingly written.

7. Have a daily program and stick to it.

8. Use the simplest language that your subject will bear. The simplest writing is the best writing because it has the widest appeal.

DON'TS FOR WRITERS

1. Don't submit a manuscript to more than one editor at a time. Making several copies and sending them out to three or four magazines at a time is unethical and can cause embarrassing situations.

2. Don't send a letter of inquiry to an editor concerning the article you would like to send him. Send it instead!

3. Don't write a letter of explanation when you mail your manuscript.

4. Above all, don't get discouraged when rejection slips pour in. Keep plenty of material on editors' desks; make the rejection slip serve as a challenge or a test of endurance to you. If you do that, you can't help selling before too long.

5. Don't be afraid to rewrite. Someone once aptly said, "You have not learned to write until you have learned to rewrite." Be critical of your own work, admit weaknesses you see in it, revise carefully. Don't be satisfied with anything less than the best you can do.

WHY DO WE GET REJECTIONS?

Every writer gets rejection slips, so make up your mind that you will, too. There are literally dozens of reasons why an editor rejects manuscripts, and the encouraging part of it is that sometimes it isn't the writer's fault. Here are some of them:

1. He may recently have used a similar article.
2. His budget may be exhausted.
3. Perhaps the subject isn't fitted to his needs.
4. Maybe he received it too late to publish that year. (If it were seasonal)
5. It may not be the length story or article he uses. (Your fault in slanting)
6. Maybe it doesn't tell a story.
7. It may have local interest only.
8. Insufficient interest
9. A limited appeal
10. Too wordy (too long getting nowhere)
11. Too complex a plot
12. Too "preachy"
13. Polished style, but a poor plot
14. Good plot, but a poor style
15. Weak beginning
16. Not convincing
17. Too little action
18. Slovenly manuscript

19. No punch at end
20. Characters sound counterfeit
21. Lack of realism

YOU WHO WOULD WRITE

Even the most successful authors have had their early struggles and disappointments. Someone has said, "Writing is a decidedly fascinating uphill fight." And that expresses most aptly how the beginning writer may feel on many occasions. But it does also imply that there are at least three rules we should heed if we're going to come through: Work hard. Be patient. Don't quit.

Remember that Booth Tarkington wrote constantly for eight years and earned exactly $22.50; that Louis Bromfield wrote four unpublished novels before his "first" one, *The Green Bay Tree*, was sold in 1924; that Zona Gale has always written, yet records show that for nine years she was writing stories and submitting them persistently to magazines before one was accepted in 1904. Furthermore, Joseph Hergesheimer, after years of struggle, had his first manuscript accepted by *Good Housekeeping*. It was a stuffed cabbage recipe published in his wife's name!

See what we mean? Don't quit!